BFI Modern Classics

Rob White
Series Editor

BFI Modern Classics is a series of critical studies of films produced over the last three decades. Writers explore their chosen films, offering a range of perspectives on the dominant art and entertainment medium in contemporary culture. The series gathers together snapshots of our passion for and understanding of recent movies.

Forthcoming

(see a full list of titles in the series
at the back of this book)

Distant Voices, Still Lives
Paul Farley

Bombay

Lalitha Gopalan

 Publishing

For Itty

First published in 2005 by the
British Film Institute
21 Stephen Street, London W1T 1LN

The British Film Institute promotes greater
understanding and appreciation of,
and access to, film and moving image
culture in the UK.

Series design by Andrew Barron
& Collis Clements Associates

Typeset in Italian Garamond
and Swiss 721BT by
D R Bungay Associates,
Burghfield, Berks

Printed in the UK by
Cromwell Press, Trowbridge, Wiltshire

British Library Cataloguing-in-Publication Data
A catalogue record for this book is available
from the British Library

ISBN 0–85170–956–7

Contents

Acknowledgments

Goodwill has infused this project from its inception. In hindsight, Thotta Tharani's gift of drawings of the set he was designing for *Bombay* in 1994 was a fortuitous beginning. Mani Ratnam was generous with interview time and unstinting with access to resources on the film. At Madras Talkies, U. V. Pani's meticulous records eased the process of assembling various materials. Rajiv Menon and Srinivas Bhashyam's skills as raconteurs transformed incidents during film shooting into an adventure narrative. Interviews with Ramgopal Varma and Chetan Shah were crucial in constructing the history of the Steadicam in India.

Naman Ramachandran's advice on the film struck the right note. Thanks to Nasreen Munni Kabir for sharing her file on *Bombay* and to Krishna Gopalan for locating obscure reports. Chris Berry and Jeannette Paulson Hereniko's invitation to the Global/Local/Exotics symposium in Hawaii provided the ideal testing ground for my ideas. Thanks to Elisa Diehl for copy-editing and to the staff at Georgetown University's Gelardin Center for downloading the appropriate images. At the BFI, Tom Cabot pulled out all the stops in the final stages.

Rob White's contribution to the project remains immeasurable and he much deserves his reputation as a film scholar's dream editor.

Introduction

One film recalls another. I attended the screening of Elia Suleiman's *Divine Intervention* (2002) in Washington, DC, savouring its wildly entertaining experiments in narrating the story of a nation continually under siege. A fragmentary narrative that declares the impossibility of telling the straightforward story of Palestine, the film demands that we consider the implicit links between narrative cinema and the history of a nation. In this witty riposte to dominant conventions of narrative cinema that raids a global archive of visual and aural permutations, an Indian film makes an auspicious entry into the film. The protagonist, whose peripatetic journeys through the militarised areas of Palestine produce many a visual flight, approaches a checkpoint; the soundtrack plays the theme music from Mani Ratnam's *Bombay* (1995). Whether Suleiman was aware of it or not, the melancholic strains from *Bombay*, composed by music director A. R. Rahman, hit the perfect note in *Divine Intervention*. The soundtrack, underscoring the never-ending antagonisms between the Israeli state and the aspirations of the Palestinians, is in no uncertain terms a divine interlude. The closing credits reveal that Rahman's music has found its way into a collection of global music, reducing my epiphany to pedantry. But that revelation cannot stop my cinephiliac desire to detect an uncanny kinship between the two films. *Divine Intervention* forces me to remember *Bombay* and its evocation of the traumatic events that rocked the nation and the city of Mumbai after Hindu fundamentalists razed the historic Babri Masjid on 6 December 1992.

Divine Intervention beckons us to consider *Bombay* as one of a growing number of films – produced in such places as Macedonia, Hong Kong, and Palestine – that battle with the fraught relationship between narration and national trauma. Such a categorisation has already enabled *Bombay*'s wide circulation. It was screened in over twenty international film festivals, including Cannes in 1995, and in the special section 'Film from the South' at the Oslo Film Festival, 2002. It also earned the Gala Award at the Edinburgh Film Festival (1995) and the Wim Van Leer in Spirit of

Freedom Award at the Jerusalem International Film Festival in Israel (1995).[1] On the national stage, *Bombay* received several awards in 1995 endorsing its landmark status: the national award for the Best Film on National Integration, and Suresh Urs for editing; Filmfare and Screen-Videocon Awards for Best Director; Cinema Express Awards for Best Picture, Best Director, Best Actor (Arvind Swamy), Best Actress (Manisha Koriala), Best Playback Female Singer (K. S. Chitra) and Best Lyric Writer (Vairamuthu).

These national and international awards underline *Bombay*'s privileged place in global cinema as a modern classic. But this view is only a partial reading and is slightly at odds with its original reception. Controversy dogged the film before and after its release in India, marking it as the most anxiously awaited and most damned film to hit the Indian screen in years. This essay will revisit the furore surrounding the film's production and first release by piecing together the film-maker's stormy interactions with the Board of Censors and the public's responses to the film's allegedly controversial content. However vociferous and unflattering the responses, they tended to cast the film in exceptional terms, as if *Bombay* were a singularly different film; that it was one of hundreds of popular films made in India and may exhibit features of other genres barely surfaced in the reviews. The attempt here is not to offer an unrestrained revisionist reading but to entertain the possibility that after a decade since its release, the film might be available for another kind of framing, a framing that may highlight its popularity, both nationally and internationally. I do not wish to underplay the significance of the early volatile responses to the film but would like to reconsider *Bombay*'s genre status by suggesting that its visualisation of traumatic social and political events has more in common with quintessentially genre films than its early reception permitted us to see. When coupled with the love story, *Bombay* bears close resemblance to a subgenre of horror films that is predicated on exploiting certain unresolved issues in public consciousness. Such a recasting of the film's narrative structuring permits us to assess how it reinterprets genres, available globally, by assimilating them with conventions of Indian popular cinema, and how in the process of finessing local and global conventions we can discern a director's style.

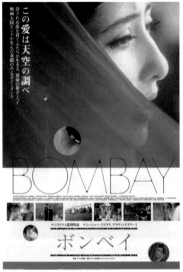
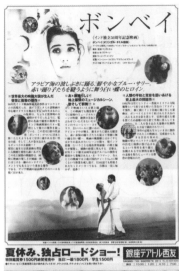

Mani Ratnam, the primary author of *Bombay*, is India's most successful popular film-maker and his films travel regularly to international film festivals. The release of one of his films is a charged event. As with most biographies that are part fact, part fiction, Ratnam's, too, is short on details but long on myth. Among the particulars, which suggest that he was raised in a liberal milieu, we learn that his father was a film distributor in Madras and that a brother, G. Venkateshwaran, launched G. V. Films and bailed Ratnam out when he experienced financial woes during the production of *Nayakan/The Hero* (1987) by persuading Sujata Films to complete its production. Ratnam's degree in management from Bajaj Management School is often cited to explain his tremendous success at the box office or his ability to manage efficiently various aspects of film production. On the domestic front, his marriage to actress Suhasini has resulted in productive collaborations: they co-wrote the scripts for his *Iruvar/The Duo* (1997) and for her *Indira* (1996).

Ratnam's first two films, which rarely surface in the international retrospectives showcasing his work, are nearly impossible to locate.

Poster for *Bombay* from the Tokyo International Film Festival

Although it is difficult to see Ratnam as anything but a director based in Madras who makes occasional forays into the Hindi market, he started his career by shooting the film *Pallavi Anupallavi* (1983) in Kannada, starring Anil Kapoor, Kiron and Lakshmi. His desire to work in Kannada was dictated by an interest in alternative forms of storytelling that distinguished Kannada New Wave cinema of the 1970s and 1980s. Having heard mere snippets of the film's plot from less than reliable sources, I can venture to say only that it revolves around a marriage. Ratnam's only comment about this film is on the choice of Anil Kapoor, who was already a star and seemed embarrassed to have had a major role in a flop. Obviously, as with moral tales about reversals of fortunes, it is Ratnam who holds the cards.

His second film, *Unaru* (1984), starring Mohan Lal, deals with labour unrest in Kerala. Surprisingly, both domestic and political themes surface repeatedly, as if he is still working through certain kinks of his earlier films. He has not yet explained his almost permanent migration to Tamil films, but there is no doubt that, earlier on, he had no desire to be locked into one regional film industry. In that respect, he is not unique: there has always been a migration of directors, actors and technicians between the different southern industries. Prior to these two films, Ratnam collaborated on a film about the Kolar gold mines that was never completed. In hindsight, it is clear that his early years are very much the stuff of myth that tails any prodigious director whose beginnings provide a glimpse of several unrealised possibilities.

When I interviewed Ratnam in 2002, he facetiously commented that he had probably started making films because of the poor production quality of Tamil films. And it is in the Tamil film industry that he has made a place for himself by initially forging a tight relationship with cinematographer P. C. Sriram and art director Thotta Tharan. Their partnership boasts of such successes as *Mouna Ragam/Silent Symphony* (1986), *Agni Nakshtram/Clash* (1988), *Geetanjali* (1989) and *Anjali* (1990). *Nayakan* emerged as an early classic that earned several awards, making it both a critical and a commercial success. However, it was the brouhaha caused by *Roja* (1992) that expanded his audience.

Enthusiastically received by the public and lambasted by critics, *Roja*
catapulted Ratnam to the national and global stage in a way that none of
his earlier works had foreshadowed.

Stories abound about how Ratnam was mobbed at Alyque Padamsee's
advertising office on a research trip for *Bombay*. The office staff was eager
to catch a glimpse of the director from Madras who had outshone Bombay
film-makers with the release of *Roja*.[2] By the time *Bombay* was ready for
release, Bombay-based film journalists like Bhawna Somaya – editor of *g*
magazine – seemed to be familiar with Ratnam's output recognising
recurring motifs in his films such as 'rain shots against lighting' and how
'All decisive moments of your characters get resolved at dusk.'[3] Despite his
success in the Hindi market, Ratnam considers Madras his primary base
and he continues to produce and direct films in Tamil. Hence, it is not
surprising that, after the tremendous success of *Bombay*, Ratnam's next
film was the magnum opus *Iruvar* in Tamil, or that, after the critical failure
of *Dil Se/From the Heart* (1998), he made two small films in Tamil about
marriage and family: *Alaipayuthey/Waves* (2000) and *Kannathil
Muthamittal/A Peck on the Cheek* (2002). To date, Ratnam has directed
seventeen films, two of which *Ayutha Ezhuthu* and *Yuva*, were shot
simultaneously, one in Tamil and one in Hindi – different cast, same story.

Despite enjoying commercial success, Ratnam has had to acknowledge
the advantage of financing his own films – *Nayakan* was nearly derailed
when Muktha Films withdrew its support. The various production
companies he has launched, including XYZ, with Shekhar Kapoor and
Ramgopal Varma, to produce *Dil Se*, point to the rather precarious process
of securing financing in India, which at times evokes images of fly-by-night
operations and shifty speculators. Most directors, including Ratnam,
Varma and J. P. Dutta, have preferred to establish and maintain control
over their own production as a way of mitigating the vagaries of financial
capital. The largely unexpected national success of *Roja*, which filled the
coffers of the Hindi producer Babu H. Shah and the Tamil producer K.
Balachander, may have motivated Ratnam to produce his own films or, at
least, to take charge of the production process, as he finally did for
Nayakan. In partnership with S. Sriram, a former classmate from Bajaj

Management School, Ratnam launched Aalayam Productions, the company that produced *Thiruda! Thiruda!* (1993) and *Bombay*. With *Iruvar*, he embarked on Madras Talkies, a production outfit that has occasionally subsidised film production for select former assistants.

Bombay belongs to a group of four films directed by Ratnam, starting with *Roja* and currently ending with *Kannathil Muthamittal*, that grapples with social and political antagonisms: communal strife in *Bombay*; secessionist movements in Kashmir in *Roja*; guerrilla movements of the north-east in *Dil Se*; and the civil war in Sri Lanka in *Kannathil Muthamittal*. Although these political events provide a spectacular canvas for nationalist melodramas enticing national and global audiences, they are also noteworthy for the ways in which Ratnam adeptly intertwines topical events with marriage plots or love stories to produce winning combinations of desire and power.

Although *Bombay* seems secure in this category, the initial spark for the script reveals other possibilities. Srinivas Bhashyam, one of Ratnam's assistant directors on Bombay (cited as T. B. Srinivas in the closing credits), recalls listening to him narrate a story of two runaways from Tamil Nadu who find themselves caught up in the midst of riots. It is a narrative direction that seems similar to one of his other films: *Nayakan*. As is often the case with the scriptwriting process, the commercially attractive tale of a Hindu–Muslim marriage set against the backdrop of violence won out over the simpler tale of masculine distress. Whatever compelled Ratnam to depict a Hindu–Muslim marriage, there is no doubt that the violence that ignited Bombay in 1992 and 1993 was the impetus for both narratives.

Bombay traces the love story of a Hindu man, Shekhar, and a Muslim woman, Shaila Banu, who meet in the fictional village of Maanguddi in Nellai District, in southern India (the Hindi version calls the village Malampur). Facing opposition from both sets of parents, Shekhar leaves his village for Bombay, sending for Shaila Banu a short time later. It is in Bombay that they marry and have twin sons, Kamal and Kabir, and it is also in Bombay that they face the rise of the communal tensions that marked the social fabric of India in the 1980s and 1990s. Communal riots in Bombay, provoked by the demolition of the Babri Masjid by Hindu fundamentalists in December 1992, splinter the family. A miraculous reunion between parents and children also allows for an intergenerational rapprochement: Shekhar's father and Shaila Banu's parents arrive in Bombay and are reconciled with their estranged children. Another round of riots in January ruptures the short-lived reunion, killing or scattering various members of the family: Shaila and Shekhar's parents die in communal fires and the twins are separated from each other and from their parents. As Bombay burns, Shekhar and Shaila Banu hunt for their children, only to be reunited with them at the very moment the leaders of the Hindu and Muslim communities call a halt to the insane marauding.

Aside from the frisson caused by a Hindu–Muslim romance and marriage that is scarcely seen in Indian cinema, *Bombay* offered Ratnam a chance to rework the city's photogenic allure that has been so widely captured on screen. Its colonial gothic facades are ideal establishing shots in social melodramas; its long beaches provide inviting sets for romantic scenes; its crowded suburban trains and buses set the scene for office romances in smaller films or for chase sequences; its nightscapes present a fitting playground for gangsters, who often wind through the city's labyrinth of alleys; its clubs and bars establish the city's gangster credentials with scenes of shootouts and dancing molls in crime films; and its slums provide gritty realism for socially committed film-makers.[4]

Ratnam was not immune to the city's picturesque possibilities, having used its gothic buildings in his gangster film *Nayakan*. However, it was not to celebrate the city's iconic landmarks that he returned, but to record the communal riots that besieged Bombay in 1992–3 and dashed his images of his city as a model secular site: 'Bombay was the biggest hope for a secular and cosmopolitan India.'[5] *Bombay* was not singular in its attempt to re-enact the riots; a number of documentary film-makers deployed their cameras to record the violence firsthand. Nor did the film inaugurate a significant shift in genre, yet its force in public memory seems over-determined.[6] By the time *Bombay* was completed and ready for viewing in 1995, the city had undergone another transformation: the right-wing Hindu nationalist party, the Shiva Sena, exercising its clout after securing a victory in the state elections, changed its name from Bombay to Mumbai.

During April and May 1995, a casual bystander wandering through the city watched with dread and curiosity all the trappings of high theatre, in which the main attraction was a face-off between cinema and politics: as the letters of Mumbai made a brash entrance over government buildings across the city, hoardings of Ratnam's *Bombay* mounted on billboards, clung to another history. For the outsider, the film's title carries a faint whiff of anachronism, while for those in the know, it dates the rise and establishment in the city of the militant right-wing Hindu parties. For Ratnam, the lure of the city has always been in its name and, even during production, he 'did not have alternative titles. It was always *Bombay*.'[7]

1 Production, Censorship and Reception

Toward the end of 1993, Ratnam went to Bombay to learn firsthand the magnitude of the riots. The trip included long conversations with Padamsee, who played an active role in the formation of Citizens for Peace, a spontaneous response to the riots; Asghar Ali Engineer, who has devoted many years to keeping alive the idea of a secular India; as well as other community leaders from the English-speaking sections of Bombay, whose secular aspirations have been betrayed, and, in effect, propelled several of them to initiate various peace-keeping efforts.

Ratnam also visited Dharavi, Asia's largest slum and the setting of *Nayakan*, to meet the poorest and hardest-hit victims of the riots. Listening to the victims' accounts, it was slowly becoming clear to him that there was no consistent story about the rampant violence. Several of them had not only suffered aggression but also had not hesitated to retaliate. In a small way, the inability of the victims either to take full responsibility or categorically blame a certain segment of society surfaces as a predicament in the film. In the final reckoning, the film remains a liberal response to the Bombay riots, blaming both Hindus and Muslims equally without ever recognising the societal inequalities that mark Hindus as the dominant population group and Muslims as the beleaguered and economically disadvantaged minority.

Although Ratnam encountered a cross-section of Bombay on this trip, he did not meet with members of the Shiv Sena, which had unabashedly admitted targeting Muslims. The party's interests in the film would adversely affect its release, but that story will have to wait to be told.

Several of his encounters and stories from this trip obtained in the film: Dileep Padgaonkar, the journalist who had persevered in providing the detailed accounts of the riots that eventually emerged as the founding document for civil rights activists and the courts, was undoubtedly a thinly disguised model for the character Shekhar; and a police officer who had shown impartiality with the marauding mobs and had not been afraid to prevent them from committing further acts of violence became the model for the harried officer who tries to defend his position when interrogated by Shekhar after the first blast.

Besides trying to document stories, Ratnam was piecing together the visual look of the city in the aftermath of the riots. In keeping with this idea, the yellow hues that had evoked the 1950s in *Nayakan* were replaced by the colour palate that he conceived for *Bombay*: serene blues to open the film in southern India, vibrant reds for the volatile Bombay cityscape, black for the riot-infested parts of the narrative, and a slow change from black to blue as reconciliation takes place. In addition to composing the colour scheme, Ratnam also borrowed from the vivid, yet melancholic, images of news photography: the abandoned car, the twisted metal, the gutted buildings and the forgotten corpses, whose images appeared on the covers of national newspapers and were subsequently collected in Padgaonkar's book.[8] While news photographs served as a primary source for the visualisation of violence, Ratnam was also aware of the documentary films that had sprung from these events and recorded with great vigilance the violent events of December 1992 to March 1993. Among the films that confronted hostile mobs, who had little compunction about destroying film equipment or attacking the photographer, Ratnam was drawn to Suma Josson's *Bombay's Blood Yatra* (1993) as emblematic of the on-the-ground reporting of the riots.

Armed with details, both visual and narrative, Ratnam returned to Madras to start production. Although the film was about Bombay, Ratnam constructed his set in Madras, where he could exercise greater control; at the end of shooting, he had spent only three or four days in Bombay. Once again, he called on his art director, Thotta Tharani, who had helped create the Bombay cityscape for *Nayakan*, to erect a set on an empty lot of the Campa Cola estates in Guindy. For 30 lakhs of rupees, Tharani produced extensive sketches of a Bombay neighbourhood, with shops squeezed next to each other, apartment dwellings standing cheek by jowl, layers of clothes hanging out to dry from every window and balcony, and a frenzied collection of billboards. It is to this Bombay that Shekhar wants to escape from his bucolic village, and it is this Bombay that welcomes Shaila. Although the set Tharani constructs for *Bombay* is not the large slum that

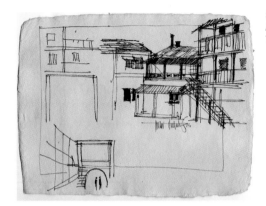

Sketches of the set for
Bombay by art director
Thotta Tharani

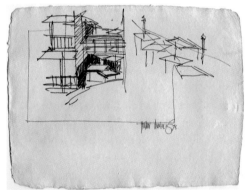

we see in *Nayakan*, it is still close to the red-light district, an economically precarious neighbourhood inhabited by sex workers, immigrants from the south and Hindu fundamentalists – a ragbag of characters who surround Shaila and Shekhar's home.

While the sprawling grounds of the Campa Cola factory were ideally suited for the street and neighbourhood scenes, Ratnam chose an abandoned building in the Express Estates, also in Madras, for the interior shots of Shekhar and Shaila's apartment (when the building was torn down in December 2003, obituaries recalled its role in Ratnam's films). The Indo-Sarcenic architecture in the Express Estates, with its tall columns and high ceilings, appears in several of his films, including as Nayakan's home and as the hospital in *Alaipayuthey*. In a delightful play of spatial discontinuity, Ratnam used the interiors of a house on the perimeter of Madras for the scenes in Shaila's family home; an impressive feudal mansion in Pollachi, seen in the Tamil film *Thevar Magan* (1992), as Shekhar's parents' home; and Kasargod for the opening scenes in the fictitious village of Maanguddi, whose causeway and bridge appear once again in *Alaipayuthey*. Ratnam is not alone in creating a diegesis in the form of a geographical jigsaw puzzle; film-makers have long been aware that continuity in cinema need not be limited by a theatrical *mise en scène*; the cut can transport us from Kasargod to Pollachi without missing a beat of Shekhar's desire.

It was logical to invite cinematographer Santosh Sivan, who had filmed *Roja* and seemed to exhibit a particular sensitivity, to convert topical issues into saleable commercial ventures. But Sivan was shooting *Indira* (1995), directed by Suhasini, Ratnam's wife, and was unavailable for this assignment.[9] However, choosing a substitute for Sivan was less than straightforward. In the search for an actor to play Shekhar, Ratnam screen-tested Rajiv Menon, a successful cinematographer who ran his own advertising firm, RM Productions, in Madras. However flattering it is to play the hero in a popular film, Menon preferred to pitch for the role of the cinematographer, a career for which he had trained at the Madras Film Institute, and he successfully managed to convince Ratnam of his intentions. Like Sivan, Menon launched his own directorial career after

Director Mani Ratnam and cinematographer Ravij Menon on the set of *Bombay*

working with Ratnam directing *Minsara Kanavu/Electric Dreams* (1997) and *Kandukondain Kandukondain/I have seen you* (2000).

Once recruited, Menon had his own ideas for this project. He wanted his cinematography to look distinctly different from Ratnam's longstanding and successful collaboration with P. C. Sriram, which featured backlighting and was dominated by framed doorways and the colours of dusk. Inspired by the documentation and re-creation of the Vietnam War, Menon took for his models *Apocalypse Now* (1979) and *The Killing Fields* (1984) to convey a 'heightened sense of reality' that was horrifying yet would be 'stunning and beautiful'.[10] Some of the images of the police action in India were also imprinted on his mind: roads littered with slippers, pools of blood on the tarmac, burning tyres, white and black smoke clogging the air. All of these images governed the visual grammar of violence in *Bombay*, making it, according to the well-known cinematographer, Ashok Mehta, visually one of the best films, and yet one that surprisingly failed to garner many awards.

Violent film scenes invariably create their own casualities, and *Bombay* racked up a few despite the special-effects technicians on board. Even before the shoot began, Menon had an accident while hunting for a location: he slipped and fell on a monsoon-drenched path in Kasargod, incurring a deep gash to his forehead. For most of the shoot, a bandage

Mani Ratnam directing Arvind Swamy in *Bombay*

hampered his sight in one eye. More accidents followed for the crew once shooting began: Menon fell over the crane and found himself dangling from a dangerous height; in one of the riot sequences, a bayonet sliced the face of the focus puller, Gaja, who was trying to get a better shot; an actor burned his thighs while trying to smother swiftly moving flames in one of the scenes. These accidents, none of which was mentioned in reviews of the film were recounted with relish by cinematographers as survival stories and the occupational hazards of the profession.

Having lined up a cinematographer, Ratnam next turned to casting the characters. Mahima Choudhury was briefly in the running for the role of Shaila Banu, but Manisha Koirala was a stronger contender. Koirala had recently earned critical attention for her performance in *Saudagar* (1991), particularly from cinematographer Anil Mehta, who recommended her to Menon. She flew to Madras for a screen test, and Menon's still photographs convinced Ratnam that Koirala was a perfect fit for Shaila Banu. For the part of Shekhar, Ratnam now looked no further than Arvind Swamy, whom he had cast in *Roja*. The hunt for the twin boys was resolved in Hyderabad, where the two young actors had appeared in a couple of commercials. Unlike the vast number of children who have appeared in Ratnam's films, this pair of twins did not care for acting and reportedly spent most of their time during the shoot revelling in the successes of their favourite Indian cricketers Sachin Tendulkar and Vinod Kambli. One of the boys was more receptive to direction, and Ratnam did not hesitate in using him as a body double for his brother in the more emotionally challenging scenes. Several members of the supporting cast were recruited from Ratnam's stable of regular actors – among them Krishnamurthy, or Kitty, who appeared in *Agni Nakshtram* and Nasser and Tinnu Anand, who acted in *Nayakan*. Others, like Prakash Raj, would appear again in *Iruvar*.

Although Ratnam's storytelling style is heavily linear, his shooting process is more scrambled, straightened out later in the editing room. For instance, the shooting of *Bombay* began in 1994 with scenes in the couple's flat in Bombay followed by scenes of rioting. The film crew then headed to Kasargod in Kerala during the monsoons in June and July to shoot the opening sections of the film, to Bekal Fort for the song 'Uyire', and to Madurai to shoot the wedding song at the Tirumala Nayak palace. A short trip to Bombay with a small crew yielded a few images for the 'Hula Bula' song as well as the establishing shots that punctuate the film. The shooting ended in Ooty with the 'Kuchi Kuchi Rakamma' song. In seven or eight months, Ratnam averaged a shooting ratio of 1:5 film footage, which he regularly edited between shoots, allowing him to have a print ready for release in Tamil, Telugu and Hindi in December 1994. But a series of events involving the Board of Censors in Madras and Bombay, protests from communal groups and instructions from the police delayed the film's release until April 1995.

Roja's success ensured advance publicity for *Bombay*, although some of it was unsolicited. Manisha Koirala had allegedly revealed bits of the plot to a reporter, ignoring Ratnam's wish to keep it secret. Of course, in reprimanding the actress for compromising the film's release, Ratnam sparked even more talk. And then there is the notorious story involving the Shiv Sena chief, Bal Thackeray, who had got wind of the plot and was incensed when he learned that the actor Tinnu Anand was playing a character based on him – the head of Shakti Samaj, a right-wing Hindu party in the film. When Anand arrived in Bombay after shooting in Madras, Thackeray's bodyguards whisked him away to debrief him. Thackeray would play a significant role in the film's post-production phase, demanding changes and exercising his authority as the head of the powerful Shiv Sena. But we are getting ahead of ourselves, at least a little.

Ratnam, normally a reluctant interviewee, was suddenly granting rather lengthy interviews to film magazines before the release of the film in an attempt to dispel wild rumours that he had completed a project about the bomb-blasts that had shaken the city in January 1993. According to Somaya, he had even retained the services of a public relations officer (Gopal Pandey) to arrange the advance publicity for *Bombay*. In one interview published in late 1993, Ratnam offers the following explanation for suddenly courting the press:

Many people have been given to understand that *Bombay* is about bomb-blasts. I just want to say it is a film about two people, and the riots just form the background of the movie. In fact, no bomb-blasts appear in my film. People have said that it is a controversial film and blah blah blah ... Such a thing has never happened with my earlier films. Nothing was ever spoken about the script. I've never faced such a problem earlier. All these canards are being spread by a lot of people who do not even know anything about *Bombay*. So I am meeting the press only to dispel all the myths about the movie. And just to tell the people that my film is going to be released, and it is a genuine attempt by a film-maker to bring about communal harmony.[11]

Despite these attempts to manage *Bombay*'s reception, I doubt Ratnam anticipated the prolonged negotiations with the Board of Censors or the politicians who were wielding the instrument of censorship to demand several cuts. Let us try to piece together this story.

According to the reporters of *Sunday*, who wrote from Hyderabad, Bangalore and Madras, Ratnam submitted *Bombay* to the Board of Censors in Madras for routine certification on 25 December, 1994.[12] The regional officer, who had recently taken charge, assured Ratnam that the film would receive a U certificate – a universal certificate without stipulations. But, overnight, the officer rescinded the rating and recommended three major cuts. Ratnam refused, and the officer sent the film to the Bombay office instead of setting up a tribunal to hear the director's defence. There is no doubt that as the film was also being released in Hindi, the Board of Censors in Bombay may have had its own recommendations. However, given bureaucratic sentiments over turf, it is routine to accept the rulings of one office, and, in this case, the Madras office would have been the first to issue the certificate for the Tamil version. Ratnam attributes the Board of Censors attempts at foot-dragging to the approaching elections in Maharashtra, in which the Shiv Sena was favoured in what looked like a strong swing towards the Hindu right.[13] By now, a whiff of trouble hung over the film, marking it as controversial. The film passed through ten different levels of committee before the Board of Censors passed a ruling.

When the film arrived at the Bombay office, the chairman of the Board of Censors, Shakti Samanta, a film-maker who has done his own share of dodging the Board of Censors with risqué scenes, decided against any immediate rulings, preferring instead to solicit the opinion of the police. According to reporters, the screening for the police force was encouraging: only one officer voted against releasing the film. Despite this endorsement from the police, the Board of Censors decided that it was more appropriate for the Home Department in the State of Maharashtra to judge the film. However, that office, too, sought the advice of a higher department, and the film found its way to the office of the Chief Minister of Maharashtra, Sharad Pawar. In what can only be described as pre-election jitters, the film was shuttled out of Pawar's office to the Home Ministry in Delhi, spending two months moving from one office to another.

Certificate from the Madras film censor's board

At this point, the producers, Aalayam Productions and S. Sriram, were flatly told that the film would have to wait until after the elections and would, of course, be subject to censorship. Again and again, Ratnam heard from members of the board and from the police that the Indian public was not ready for a Hindu–Muslim romance; one police commissioner, in fact, insisted that the film could not be released for another ten years. While it seems a bit extreme to demand such a change in the script at this point in the post-production process, the other recommended cuts were more specific and pointed: footage depicting kar sevaks demolishing the Babri Masjid, which was filmed by the BBC and widely televised in India; shots of a woman hit by a stray bullet and falling over her balcony; references to Pakistan in the dialogue; and footage of the police shooting into the crowds. All in all, the censors insisted on cutting only 120–150 feet of the film or, as Ratnam nonchalantly declared, 'the censors must have cut hardly two minutes of the entire film'.[14] Perusing the recommendations of the Board of Censors (see the Appendix), it is clear that the recommendations tended to protect the police from allegations of partiality and of excessive force, and, in effect, implied that the Muslims' response to the Hindu right for demolishing Babri Masjid had been unwarranted. Despite Ratnam's claims that the cuts did not tamper with the narrative flow of the film, there is no doubt that the need to place blame or to understand the motivation of the riots now seems more arbitrary than should have been necessary in a narrative film. At the same time, it must be said that rather than protest against censorship and risk having his film banned, Ratnam accepted the recommendations.

But, as with all negotiations between the state and film producers in the 1990s, *Bombay* too had to contend with the extraordinary powers of the Hindu right in what can only be characterised as a slow erosion of civil society, most evident in the dismantling of the legitimate process of statecraft, which was superseded either by the military and state police forces or by vigilantes. Hence, it comes as no surprise that it was not enough for producers to be granted carte blanche by the Board of Censors and police protection during screenings; they had to contend with the organised underworld as well as receive the tacit support of Bal Thackeray, whose power to incite riots is now legendary. A different cast now enters the story.

Ratnam and Aalayam sold the rights to the negatives of the Hindi version of *Bombay* to Amitabh Bachchan Corporation Limited (ABCL) – a film distribution company founded by the superstar Amitabh Bachchan – for 1.5 crores of rupees. According to *Sunday*, 'With other earnings, Ratnam stood to make up to Rs 2.5 crores from the Hindi version alone – not a bad deal, given that *Bombay* couldn't have cost more than Rs 3 crores to make.'[15] This arrangement between the Hindi film superstar and a star director was, according to *Sunday*, more calculated than a simple equation of money: 'it [*Bombay*] needs the backing of somebody with the clout and stature of Amitabh Bachchan'.[16] The run-ins with the censors were beyond the scope of ABCL, but, *Sunday* notes, it was 'Bachchan who arranged a special show of the movie at Prakash Mehra's Sumeet preview theater for Bal Thackeray'.[17] Here is Thackeray's reaction to the film. To say that it left the film-makers flummoxed is an understatement.

When I saw the film,' Thackeray told *Sunday*, 'I realized that Mr Tinnu Anand had portrayed me in a manner that did not reflect the truth. At the end of the riots, they show Tinnu Anand – that is, me – going around in a car. Then, when he sees the violence, he covers his face in his hands and repents. This is wrong. Totally wrong. I never repented. Why should I repent? We didn't start the violence. If you look carefully at the film, you will find that it is all there. The murder of the Mathadi workers. The burning of the house in Jogeshwari. We had no choice but to retaliate. So how can you show me repenting?[18]

A peculiar compromise between insisting, on the one hand, that the film is a fictional rendition of the riots and, on the other, that it faithfully re-creates them played itself out in Ratnam's response to Thackeray's objection. In the version of the film that was finally released, the remorseful voiceover accompanying the shots of Tinnu Anand's despondent gestures was excised, as Ratnam bowed, this time, to pressures from the head of Shiv Sena, the ex officio Board of Censors.

Although *Sunday* reported on perhaps the most scandalous of Thackeray's demands, Ratnam received a longer list of demands from the Sena chief:

There were a lot of things he wanted. He wanted an entire character removed; the character was not removed. He wanted it to be re-shot with some other person; we were able to convince him that it could not be done. He wanted the name changed to *Mumbai*, we said we couldn't.[19]

It is clear that Thackeray is accustomed to having his demands heeded and his every whim entertained. Given his expanding dominion, it is surprising that Ratnam managed to retain the title *Bombay*.[20]

In deferring to Thackeray, both Ratnam and ABCL appeared to be openly courting the Shiv Sena and seeking its reassurance that the film would not face another round of surprise attacks. With rumours proliferating of a private screening for Thackeray, the leaders of the Muslim community were gearing up to oppose the film, which they perceived as being tilted towards dominant Hindu sentiments and therefore not even-handed. In March 1995, a coalition government consisting of the Shiv Sena and the Bharatiya Janata Party (BJP) elected Manohar Joshi as the Chief Minister of Maharashtra. In spite of having already secured the Shiv Sena's approval, the distributors in Bombay postponed the film's release till mid-April.

Despite delays in Bombay, Ratnam proceeded to release the film in other parts of India. Although a box-office success, the film provoked riots and disturbances, creating a 'law and order' crisis that had police cordoning off theatres, using sniffer dogs to check for bombs, and deploying officers in riot gear to take up positions outside the cinemas where the film was being screened. With a large Muslim population, Hyderabad, the capital of Andhra Pradesh, was one of the epicentres of protests. A Telugu version of the film, released in Andhra Pradesh on 10 March, 1995, showed in at least thirteen theatres in the twin cities of Hyderabad and Secunderabad.[21]

There were several forms of protest: prominent members of the

Muslim community sent letters to editors of newspapers; a theatre in the old city was ransacked by viewers during a late-night screening on 11 March; police were summoned to respond to a bomb threat in a theatre on 12 March, which turned out to be a hoax; theatre owners received threatening calls demanding that the screening of the film be halted; and the president of the political party Majlis Bachao Tehrik, Chandrayanguta's legislator Mohammed Amanullah Kah and Majlis-Ittehadul-Muslimeen Salauddin Owaisi, the Member of the Legislative Assembly (MLA) for Charminar, demanded that Chief Minister N. T. Rama Rao ban the film.[22] The youth wings of the different leftist parties also weighed in, demanding an immediate withdrawal of the film. They objected to the images depicting the demolition of the Babri Masjid, the hero lifting the veil of a Muslim girl and the Muslim heroine appearing on screen without a *burqa*. Given the scale and spectrum of protests, the Hyderabad city police commissioner, V. Appa Rao, suspended the screening of the film for months 'under the Andhra Pradesh Cinema Regulation Act and the Hyderabad City Police Act, on the grounds that screening the movie was likely to cause breach of peace and create religious animosity between Hindus and Muslims'.[23] The incidents in the twin cities had a ripple effect and 'the ban was extended to two other districts: Rangareddy and Nizamabad'.[24]

In the neighbouring state of Karnataka, 'the film was banned in the twin cities of Hubli and Dharwar'.[25] When the film was finally released in Maharashtra on 6 April, riots erupted in the town of Nagpur. According to *Trade Guide*, the incidents at Smruti cinema seemed premeditated:

As scheduled, the first show at Smruti began on Thursday (6th April) at 9 a.m. but after intermission, 15–16 youths got up from their seats and shouted slogans demanding banning of the film. They went on a rampage, breaking chairs and huge glasses fitted to the foyer doors. As they stormed out of the theater, about the same number of persons standing outside joined them in burning a poster of the film in the premises of the cinema. … The estimated loss to the theater was about Rs 25,000.[26]

Although the frenzied mob went on to damage cars and buses outside the theatre, *Trade Guide* commented that the film did not provoke a similar reaction at Alankar, the other theatre in Nagpur. Police and film distributors exercised restraint in Bhopal, Gujarat, by postponing the release of the film by a week after securing the approval of officials and 'prominent citizens'.[27]

When the film was finally scheduled for a public screening in Bombay, the stakes were extremely high, the air was fraught with tension and polarised views dominated its reception. Bachchan allegedly received threats on his life. That the producers had solicited Thackeray's approval did not escape the notice of the Muslim community, which was still recovering from the communal riots of December 1992 and January 1993. Instead of waiting for the freshly installed coalition government to protect their interests, which, given the swing to the Hindu right, was highly unlikely, the leaders of the Muslim community took matters into their own hands. Led by G. M. Banatwalla, leader of the Indian Union Muslim League, they protested outside the theatre on the day of the film's release. Banatwalla declared that 'the film reportedly shows the Muslim community as arrogant and hostile'.[28] Instead of passing a blanket judgment on the film, other representatives of the Muslim community chose a more studied form of protest. Raza Academy General Secretary Ibrahim Tai, Muslim League Corporator Yusuf Abrahani and others organised a special screening at the New Excelsior theatre on 6 April. According to *Trade Guide*, security at the event was heavy:

Before the commencement of the screening, the bomb squad of the city police checked all the seats with the help of sniffer dogs. A couple of hours before the film was shown to the select audience, the police threw a cordon around the theater. All the approach roads were also manned by lathi and rifle-wielding policemen. Moreover, all vehicles in the vicinity of the theater were checked while some of them were even towed away.' [29]

Conferring with the police 'on the top floor of the theater', the leaders were unanimous in their verdict that the film was 'anti-Islamic'. *Trade*

Guide reported that the film could well open wounds in the Muslim community: of the 700 killed in the communal riots in 1992 and 1993, the majority were Muslims, who made up only 9.5 per cent of the city's population (the statistics vary widely; these are from *Asian Age*, 4 April, 1995). Muslim leaders particularly objected to the scene depicting the heroine's flight from her parents' home 'to join her Hindu lover carrying a copy of Koran in her hand while in the background, certain verses from the holy book were chanted. This scene gave the impression that Koran sanctioned the heroine's act.'[30]

Given the volatile reaction to the film by leaders of the Muslim community, Bombay Police Commissioner Satish Sawhney postponed its release until 14 April, even though tickets were sold out for shows starting on 2 April at thirteen theatres in the city. The commissioner even suggested that 'Mr Tai appeal to the Censor Board in Delhi for further deletions in the film that hurt the Muslim community's sensibilities'.[31] Tai was vehement about his objections:

'When it is obvious that Muslims all over the country are objecting, why can't the Maharashtra government see reason? If the movie is shown there will be a third riot in Bombay.' (…) Mr Tai said that even 500 policemen posted outside the cinema hall could not ensure peace if the film was released. 'The message of the film is not clear. Only in the last 10 minutes, the two communities are shown protecting each other. If a man is unclean and only his hands are washed, you wouldn't call him a clean man, would you?' asked Mr. Tai.[32]

While the postponed release may have provided much-needed negotiating time, Muslim leaders were still considering banning the film, either by approaching the high court in Bombay or the Information and Broadcasting Ministry in Delhi.[33] At the same time, the newly elected right-wing coalition in Maharashtra was fighting to have the film released, with the Chief Minister insisting that 'the picture should run. That is our feeling, it is a question of freedom of expression.'[34] The impasse continued for several days, but when it looked as if the state government was bent on releasing the film, the All India Muslim Personal Law Board launched a different tactic – to boycott the film. In addition, the board decided to use the film to 'increase awareness about Islam' and issued the following statement to the press:

The Islamic Sharia prohibits the viewing and making of films and now the film *Bombay* has given us an opportunity to start a peaceful movement in our community to create genuine awareness for complete submission to Allah's commandments and wean away every single Muslim from viewing cine films and all sorts of evils.[35]

The call to boycott the film rather than protest outside theatres or organise rallies may have caused the negotiations between the police and the leaders of the Muslim community to break down, allowing the distributors – Shrirnagar Films – to release the film in Bombay on 15 April. There is no doubt that the postponed release and the controversy surrounding the film only helped its box-office revenues. In all eleven theatres in the city, the film had sold out. The police took the precaution of bringing in additional armed police and a paramilitary force in case the film provoked any disturbances.[36]

It was now common for the theatres to be policed while the film was being shown, even in Calcutta, which did not have any protests.[37] Madras, too, remained untouched by communal sentiments, but distributors there faced a different adversary, the heavily advertised *Badshah/Emperor* (1995), produced by AVM, with the star Rajnikant in the lead. There were rumours that the distributors of *Badshah* were engaged in a dirty campaign against *Bombay*, even inciting the public to protest the film's release in other parts of the country. There were protests, but *Sunday* described one of these incidents as flippant:

In an hour, the film was sold out for the whole of the first week. The black marketers moved in and as the advance booking period of 20 days quickly filled up, tickets with a face value of Rs. 16 were being sold for Rs. 200.

This situation angered 600 students who had gone to see the movie only to find that no seats were available. On the first day of its run, they agitated outside the twin Devi-Paradise cinemas on Madras' Mount Road and when no tickets were promised, they staged a *rasta roko*.

As traffic jams clogged Mount Road, the police were sent for. But try as they might, they could not get the students to relent. 'Why was the film released clandestinely?' they asked. 'Why wasn't there any publicity?'

Finally, the police consulted with the exhibitors who agreed to hold a special show for the students. Pacified, the youths dispersed quietly and order was restored to Mount Road.[38]

Yes, the film was released, but not even its success at the box office could prevent certain incidents. On a calm morning in July, when Ratnam should have been listening to the ticking of ticket counters registering the box-office hit across India – by all accounts, he was drinking his coffee and reading the morning paper – three lead pipe bombs were hurled into his home.[39] As the police reports do not mention motives, we can only speculate that this attack against Ratnam was connected to his recent film. In Bombay, sometime in July, Manisha Koirala received threatening calls, allegedly for her role in *Bombay*, and was provided with police protection.[40]

The volatile combination of state censorship, the interference of ex officio forces, such as Bal Thackeray, and the Muslim leaders' outcry against the film ironically ensured its success at the box office. According to trade papers, in spite of competition in Hindi territory from *Hum Aapke Hain Koun/Who Am I to You?* (1994), *Bombay* was a hit, breaking several records by the end of the first week. With an eye on the box office, *Trade Guide* closed its review with praise for the film: 'On the whole, *Bombay* has terrific initial-value and contents to prove a major success.'[41] According to *Variety*, the producers distributed 268 prints on the domestic front; the international version submitted to Cannes was 102 minutes long 'shorn of the kitsch song-and-dance-interludes designed for local consumption'.[42]

Reviews of *Bombay* sprang up from unexpected quarters: political and social commentators who routinely avoided evaluating films were, nonetheless, drawn into censuring it, raising questions about Muslim identity in a society increasingly dominated by the Hindu right and about the limits of state power and authority. In some ways, this was not an unfamiliar scenario: the furore over censorship shaped the reception of Salman Rushdie's novel *Satanic Verses*, and the call to ban and censor the film *Bandit Queen* (1994) similarly came from the state as well as from the self-appointed extra-constitutional authorities. Above all, the communal riots engulfing Bombay in December 1992 and January 1993 cast doubts on the promises of secularism, particularly towards Muslims, that are guaranteed in the constitution of the post-colonial nation-state.

A perusal of reviews in the English newspapers reveals an array of positions. The daily *Asian Age*, with its national and overseas audiences, had three different reviews of the film that were united in their praise: Kavita Shanmugham reported from Madras on the film's enthusiastic reception, most prominently visible during the musical numbers;[43] Poonam Saxena was equally congratulatory, attributing courage and compassion to the director.[44] Most notably, both reviews avoided any mention of the censorship ruckus that delayed the film's release. Reporter C. Aravind launched a flattering appraisal of Ratnam's other films in the same newspaper, taking care to describe *Bombay*'s squabble with the Board of Censors.[45]

Other newspapers, however, were less than praising in their reviews of the film. Praful Bidwai's column for the *Times of India* was punchy, dismissing *Bombay* for its mediocre treatment of politics.[46] Despondent over the fuss of censorship, Bidwai asserted that 'Ratnam does not even begin to grasp the essence of January 1993 – a pogrom sustained by the collusion of the state, and the subversion of its police.'[47] He directs his ire particularly at Ratnam for allowing Hindu communalists to censor his films, implicitly inflaming Muslim communalists. The left-leaning fortnightly *Frontline* chose a different tack by commissioning two views of *Bombay*: Arun Sadhu's 'Clichés, and Beyond', an unequivocal celebration of the film, praises it for its even-handed treatment of communal riots and raves about the music;[48] Venkatesh Athreya's review, 'Bold but Distorted', offers a serious consideration of the film and its shortcomings without exacerbating the already polarised reception of the film. Without demanding that the film rework its diegesis, Athreya carefully lists the absences and silences in the film that, if corrected, would have vastly improved the final product. The first of his concerns is the film's suggestion, during the riot sequences, that the Muslims had spontaneously fomented violence after the assault on Babri Masjid. However, according to newspaper reports, the 'Shiv Sena had organized a series of "Maha aarati" rituals in various parts of Bombay to whip up anti-Muslim feeling preparatory to the planned pogrom'. What Athreya would have wanted is a comprehensive description of the tinderbox atmosphere created by the Shiv Sena in Bombay to understand the rioting in which Hindus and Muslims killed each other. According to him it is worth remembering details of the police report:

In the first round of violence in Bombay in December 1992, 202 persons were killed in 'mob violence' and police firing. Of those killed in police firing, 98 out of 132 were Muslims, and in deaths due to 'mob violence,' 32 out of 51 were Muslims. Contrast this with the fact that 14.8 per cent of Bombay's population was Muslim.

Like Bidwai, Athreya points out the film's inability to account for the brutal force of the police or their partisan disciplining that targeted Muslims, a gaping hole in the representational regime of the film that conveniently exculpates the police. His critique that the film conflates religiosity and fanaticism is pointed, even as he suggests that recommendations demanded by the censors may have scrambled the narrative logic: 'The identification of Muslim rioters by the religious cap, for instance, leaves a subtle impression that any Muslim wearing the cap is anti-Hindu. Sequences showing people in worship are immediately succeeded by scenes of violence.' Finally, Athreya comments on *Bombay*'s gender stereotyping: 'The woman, predictably, is shown as appropriately and engagingly vulnerable.'[49] Writing for the quarterly cinema journal *Deep Focus*, Georgekutty A. L. notes similarly that the film is in the grip of patriarchal codes that call for silencing women and seeking their passive assent on all matters: 'The patriarchal codes subsume and subjugate the feminine. And in that subjugation, as the patriarchal codes unfold, the secular subsumes the difference and the desired homogeneity is achieved for uninterrupted progression of the nation building project.'[50]

Resorting to a historical argument that has surfaced since the demolition of Babri Masjid, Georgekutty suggests that the shape of secularism cannot be resolved 'without an understanding of the deeper trauma of the partition of the colonial empire into India and Pakistan'.[51]

It is worth reiterating the flashpoints caused by the film's reception. Some critics quarrelled with the film's representation of Muslims as aggressive, others with its images of passive Muslim women, and yet others with its disingenuous even-handedness. Censorship authorities directed their objections to all matters concerning national security – mentions of Pakistan, scenes of police randomly firing into mobs and references to police brutality. And communal leaders, such as Bal Thackeray, exercised their ex officio powers by weighing in on particular images. Unable to counter Thackeray's domination, Muslim leaders demanded that the government ban the film, and, when dissatisfied with the state's response, they called for a boycott. Any attempt to re-read *Bombay* is so weighed down by the conditions of its initial reception that it would be foolhardy to imagine a hermeneutic exercise that could ignore the fracas and concentrate on the film qua film when the text itself has been so worked over. Yet a decade later, a reader has the right to be suspicious of the film's influence and, in effect, to evaluate the film on its own terms, even if such an exercise entails watching it alongside the admonishing voices.

2 Genre and Style

I first watched Mani Ratnam's *Bombay* at a movie theatre in Flushings, Queens, New York, where the local Tamil association had organised a Sunday morning screening in April 1995. The Hindi version had opened at the better-established Eagle and Bombay theatres, but there was only one morning screening of the Tamil version, in New York City. The theatre was packed, and three of us who had come to see the film were forced to separate, united only during the interval and at the end. So I watched the film without the pleasure, or luxury, of the whispered comments or nudges of friends. Nevertheless, it was fun to lose myself in the endless stream of comments from my fellow moviegoers, the manners we had acquired in the diaspora suspended for three hours.

My most vivid memory from that initial viewing is the scene in which Shaila Banu watches the train to Bombay, presumably the train Shekhar boarded, crossing the bridge. Striking a lovelorn pose, she looks longingly at the departing train, a gesture familiar to us from so many films in world cinema – the abandoned lover waving goodbye as the train curves out of the frame. Although there is no station in the scene and the film does not show a close-up of Shekhar's face, Shaila's gestures are no less poignant. It was not her sad face that stayed with me but the moment she leaves the frame. We are left staring at an empty space for a few frames: the

Shaila Banu arrives at Victoria terminus, Bombay

Looking for meaning: the 'open image' in *Bombay*

riverbank with a long narrow path running into the distance – the scene of the first chance encounter between Shekhar and Shaila – the same rain-washed, blue-hued landscape and the sound of the train. This was the *mise en scène* of the lovers' desire. But in a popular film that deploys characters to move the plot, this 'open image'– if not a lapse in editing – is an excessive gesture usually confined to non-commercial films or to song-and-dance sequences in commercial cinema. It dawned on me that I, too, was stranded, looking for meaning as I continued to stare at this open image – a concept put forth by Shohini Chaudhuri and Howard Finn in 'The Open Image: Poetic Realism and the New Iranian Cinema'.[52]

Although this open image of the riverbank remains etched in my memory, another image surfaced in my subsequent viewings of the film and, surprisingly, precedes in time the one with which I had developed an obsessive relationship. This second image dovetails the first song 'Kannalane/With My Eyes', which is set in the courtyard and adjoining corridors of the Tirumala Nayak palace in Madurai. Taking advantage of the gracious Indo-Sarcenic structure, Ratnam deftly employs the pillars, columned corridors and filigreed partitions between spaces as the playground for a series of hide-and-seek games between Shaila and Shekhar. Given the logic of chance meetings, this encounter, too, is set up as a surprise: Shekhar's sister forces him to accompany her to a local wedding, and he happens to spot Shaila standing in a group of girls.

The troupe of dancers nudges Shaila, dressed in a white lahenga-and-choli (skirt and blouse), with the requisite diaphanous dupatta fluttering in the breeze that she reins in at appropriate moments in this peek-a-boo dance ritual. Shaila dominates the chorus of voices – Koirala is well supported by the playback singer Chitra – seducing Shekhar while fleeing from his amorous advances. At the end of the sequence, it is abundantly clear that Shaila and Shekhar's passionate sidelong glances in the opening scene have blossomed into a consuming desire for each other. The music ends, the wedding party departs the space, and we see Shaila standing in the precise centre of a scalloped arch with the central courtyard and a row of columns and arches in the background. It is a picture-perfect moment, an ideal poster for the pretty actress, but the camera waits for her to slip out of the frame and we are left to admire this image of symmetry and excess – decorative scalloped archways arranged in a neat row. Here, too, the image appears marooned, with no particular character assignation.

Chaudhuri and Finn's formulation of the open image refers to a 'certain type of ambiguous, epiphanic image'. In a delightful reading of Pier Pasolini's, Paul Schrader's and Gilles Deleuze's tracts on cinematic time and space, they demonstrate that 'a repressed political dimension returns within the ostensibly apolitical aesthetic form of the open image'.[53] Recalling Pasolini's musings on 'free indirect subjective images' in various moments in Italian neo-realism – Antonioni's *Deserto Rosso/Red Desert* (1964) surfaces as an iconic instance – Chaudhuri and Finn remind us that, although rooted in the diegesis, these images

A 'certain type of ambiguous, epiphanic image': the open image again

cannot be straightforwardly deciphered as a revelation of either a character's psychological state or that of the film-maker. Instead the unresolved tension between the two viewpoints – character and film-maker – creates an ambiguity, a space in which the image appears to emerge from somewhere other. This 'other perspective is often, as in Antonioni's film, felt to reside in the camera itself, particularly in those scenes where the camera continues recording empty reality after people and identifiable human consciousness have departed – the camera as the uncanny eye of surveillance.[54]

Schrader's formulation of the 'transcendental style' with its focus on the 'meticulous representation of the dull, banal commonplaces of everyday living [...], an actual or potential disunity [...], and a frozen view of life' is evoked as another example of the open image.[55] Finally, Deleuze's 'time-image [...] characterized by a lack of causal links' emerges as a novel way to formulate the conceptual leaps introduced by Italian neo-realism.

Chaudhuri and Finn's resurrection of these cinematic styles to re-frame new Iranian cinema finds an uncanny resemblance to images in *Bombay*. Curiously, the two open images (the riverbank and the archway in the palace) lend themselves to the kind of reflection suggested by Schrader and imply the ambiguity expressed by Pasolini, because the human character seems to have a spurious relationship to the space of action. Yet again, the lack of causal links suggests a kinship with Deleuze's time-image. This covert genealogy is not altogether surprising given Ratnam's familiarity with world cinema and his own sense of cinematic style. A closer look at his work reveals how landscapes dominate his films with great élan, often dwarfing the characters and their movements. However, he has been careful to tie these images to the story by giving them purpose: the montage of boating scenes in the opening segment of *Bombay* sets the scene for action; nightscapes in *Nayakan* provide both the context for the action and a transit into the next segment; and the spectacular shots of Himalayan mountains in *Roja* open a sequence but quickly take a background position in relation to the heroine's point of view. There is no shortage of examples from Ratnam's oeuvre that illustrate his command of the space in which the action takes place, but these two images in *Bombay* strike us as incongruous, highlighting a moment of pure cinema in an otherwise character-driven plot.

We should not peg these open images as portentous or even eccentric flourishes of an auteur elevating the formulaic logic of popular cinema; their genius is most alluring when we consider their links to the logic of film genre. Curiously, the question of the film's genre has scarcely been a topic of elaboration, despite the force and depth of the discussions on its content. Among the various reviews and critiques of the film is one by Ravi Vasudevan, whose suggestions in his seminal essay 'Bombay and its Public' are worth amplifying.[56] Navigating carefully between the film's public reception and its textual address, Vasudevan alludes to Bombay's genre as approximating the Muslim social, films that detail a Muslim way of life. However, Vasudevan is cautious to suggest that Bombay's protracted sequences of violence, often autonomous, distract the viewer from discerning it in this way. A viewing of the film does reveal scattered intimations of this genre, most visible in scenes involving Shaila's home and the wedding song-and-dance number. However, the limited scope of the Muslim social is transposed onto a narrative of intercommunal romance that renders scenes of the Muslim household irrelevant.

Ratnam also weighed in on the film's genre affiliation, expressing himself most insistently during his tussle with the Board of Censors: 'Defending his film, Mr Ratnam told the weekly newspaper Sunday that Bombay is essentially a love story set against the backdrop of the riots: "I have made a film that speaks of the futility of violence and rioting."'[57]

Bombay undoubtedly reads like a love story but of a particular kind that rapidly morphs into the marriage plot, a recurring theme in several of his films. Additionally, 'the backdrop of riots' overwhelms the marriage story, coaxing the film into directions other than the one concerned with the trials and tribulations of a boy-meets-girl-story. Despite Ratnam's directives, the trailers that he issued, and that were widely shown on television, opened with spectacular scenes of violence, cutting to song-and-dance sequences, and then to moments from domestic sequences; the love story recedes into the background, while promises of violence are at the forefront. Between Vasudevan's charge that the sequences of violence appear autonomous and Ratnam's claim that we should see the violence as backdrop, the film has a disjointed narrative waiting to secede from itself. However, if we take another stab at describing the film's genre location, a less incoherent narrative structuring unfolds.

As viewers of genre films, we are acquainted with the endless permutations and combinations that are possible, and pride ourselves in our ability to decode covert unions between genres that even film-makers do not admit to. It is this stealth gesture that I wish to evoke and, in the process, draw attention to the shadowy presence of the horror genre in *Bombay* lurking behind the more apparent marriage story. This evocation is not as scandalous as it seems: horror films routinely deliver knotty tales of desire and sexual union in a manner that the love story is not accustomed to doing. I am prompted, here, by provocative revisionist undertakings that have elevated horror films from the lower rungs of film scholarship to centre stage with a theoretical rigour that matches the plot twists of the films.[58] These incursions have bestowed on horror films the ability to tap into our deepest fears and desires, without ever undermining the genre's deep-seated commitment to the shock effects of cinema. The ever-evolving form of horror has graduated from stacking its narratives with scientists, zombies and ghosts to signalling the unspeakable, the unrepresentable and the uncanny.

It is easy to see Ratnam's *Bombay* as a precursor to the emerging canon of horror films crowding Indian cinema with ghosts, snakes, haunted houses and tantrics.[59] Even a light-hearted comparison of *Bombay* and a boilerplate horror film reveals some curious similarities: the gloomy rain-lashed landscape that opens the film; the man mesmerised by the sight of a woman and cannot help cutting himself to express his passion (memories of fanged kisses on the neck in classical horror are close by); crowds possessed by a passion strong enough to launch marauding attacks on their neighbours; twin sons as yet another manifestation of monstrosity; and, above all, the unrepresentable union between Hindus and Muslims in popular Indian cinema. An unstoppable urge to re-evaluate Ratnam's other film in the tetralogy in this light, distorts the received wisdom that they are love stories set against the backdrop of contemporary social and political contestations: *Roja* transforms Kashmir, the preferred destination for honeymooning couples in India, into an *unheimlich* space; *Dil Se*, according to Earl Jackson Jr, is a stalker film; and *Kannathil Muthamittal*, a twisted recasting of the family romance.[60]

Although *Bombay* has several of the more obvious features of a horror film, it aspires to a closer affinity with the subgenre of films that deals with traumatic social and political events, a category that traces its roots to films by Georges Franju and Alain Resnais.[61] In these films, we find a heightened 'reality effect', where the quotidian emerges as the site of horror, such as organ donations in *Jian gui/The Eye* (2002) and environmental despair in *Safe* (1995). Repeatedly, these films complicate the spectator's relationship to the screen by soliciting our interest in a more direct way. These are the films that best prepare us to view *Bombay* by making us more aware of the 'backdrop of violence' and how it interlocks with marriage and love, an association that was obviously burnished by Ratnam's cinematographer, who was inspired by the horrific images in war films. More to the point, the open images that rupture the diegesis and invite us to anticipate the next frame are uncannily similar to the well-honed structuring of expectation in the best horror films.

A straightforward reading of these two open images would reveal them as metaphors of Shaila Banu's longing. But an irksome detail is her disappearance, her departure from the frame, which leaves us contemplating the purpose of these shots. What they do provide us with is an intimation of the 'other' waiting to burst into the frame. In his elegant reading of a similar intrusion into the frame in George Romero's *Night of the Living Dead* (1968), Ofer Eliaz persuasively argues that the zombie appears out of nowhere; an empty frame from the point of view of the protagonist Barbara is our only cue.[62] Militant Hindus, marauding mobs, burnt vehicles and massacred bodies fill the frame in rapid succession in *Bombay* once the couple reunites in the city. But it is in the distant village in southern India in which the film mobilises the initial structure of anticipation by offering us the two open images.

Although I draw attention to these open images as emerging from another scene in *Bombay*, and another genre and style, the film alerts us, more specifically, to the structuring of surprise and anticipation in the diegesis as early as the first exchange between Shekhar and Shaila. In a long shot, we see Shekhar in a red T-shirt accompanied by his companion at the riverbank. We have already seen a boat of Muslim women in *burqas* approaching the pier, a continuation of the earlier segment in which boats ferry back and forth across the river. As the women disembark and pay the boatman, we note how their long *burqas* billow in the breeze. Since we have been following Shekhar's conversation with his friend, it should come as no surprise that we mark his sudden halt with some curiosity, even if it is in long shot.

The film cuts to an extreme close-up of two hands exchanging money, breaking the rhythm of long shots and initiating a series of shot-reverse-shots. The breeze that has been swelling the *burqas* lifts up the veil covering one of the faces, and we see Shaila's face looking beyond us, at Shekhar. Weather plays a perfect partner at this moment, as it did in Guru Dutt's *Chaudvin ka chand* (1960), in which a cool breeze lifts the heroine's veil just in time for a man to fall in love with her, a film that fits quite easily into the genre of the Muslim social.[63] However, to be specific about the scene in *Bombay*, Shekhar pauses, expecting something to stir in that band of *burqa*-clad women – who we know are in the off-screen space – willing it to happen, and it does. In this case, the off-screen space seems pregnant with suspense and surprise – strange ingredients in a love story but standard fare in a horror film.

Portraying a group of Muslim women as objects of interest in the off-screen space marks them with the same mesmerising effect that we find in the hypnosis subgenre. The protagonist's fixed stare at an off-screen space has no rational explanation but is characteristic of the genre. But the effect is always double-edged: the mesmerising effect of the exotic or the ancient is equally cloaked with fear and desire of the unknown intruding into the frame from the off-screen space. Although Shekhar's interest in the off-screen emerges only through a close analysis of the shots, a version of this scene obviously angered critics: the image of a veil fluttering in the wind was tied to later scenes of Muslim mobs, recognisable by their white caps, as deplorable representations of Muslims as other.

It is worth reiterating Vasudevan's reading that *Bombay* refrains from consistently resorting to negative stereotypes of Muslims but also includes the image of the fearful Hindu, particularly emerging from the off-screen space. On a sunny day in Bombay, Shaila Banu heads into the street to post a letter to her parents, a conciliatory gesture for her secret departure. The studio set of Bombay built on the Campa Cola estates in Madras is brimming with signs of urban life. The camera is focused on Shaila who, after posting the letter, is drawn to an off-screen space, a place beyond us. Unlike in the opening segment, we have no idea what lies beyond the urban din, until the film cuts to a high-angle crane shot sweeping over a rally of saffron-clad men and their supporters chanting slogans and holding placards as they demand the construction of a temple on the site of Babri Masjid.

Muslim Shaila Banu watches a rally of Hindu fundamentalists

This scene is a direct reference to the ratha yatra (a religious chariot procession), organised by right-wing Hindu parties to whip up support for the demolition of the Babri Masjid on 6 December, 1992. At this moment in the narrative, we are still a couple of years away from that event, but the film records the rise of communalism as a fearful image from the point of view of the Muslim woman, a figure who has been at the centre of the most fraught debates on citizenship and civil rights in the last two decades. In an image of Bombay that the film suggests she was not prepared for, Shaila Banu cannot take her eyes off the procession as it passes by. It must be noted that she has already come up against a fair share of communalism during her first encounter with the couple's landlady, who mutters under her breath that Shaila Banu sounds like a Muslim name. Banu is not coy about asserting her identity as a Muslim.

Later, after the twins are born, the film evokes the fearful image of the well-documented razing of Babri Masjid by Hindu fundamentalists with the implicit support of the state. The sequence begins with an image of Babri Masjid and the caption 6 December, 1992, spliced together with superimposed shots, newspaper reports and photographs of the collapse. Towards the end of this swirl of images, we find ourselves inside the mosque as the roof slowly collapses. This benign version, which avoids identifying the perpetrators as right-wing Hindu militants, is a far cry from the version submitted to the Board of Censors, which included a re-enactment of the event, with the mob tearing down the mosque. Insisting that a replay of the images would incite further rioting, the board recommended excising the entire sequence with the exception of the photographic image of the collapse of Babri Masjid.

For my purposes here, I am particularly interested in the manner in which the film prepares us for the image. Shaila Banu responds to a solicitation at her door to find Shakti Samant soldiers – a thinly disguised image of Rashtriya Sevak Sangha (RSS) and Shiv Sena cadres – seeking donations for a temple to be erected in Ayodhya. Unable to muster a suitable response, she stands at the door till Shekhar leads the men away from the apartment. The film cuts first to Shaila at the window looking at an off-screen space on the left, and then to a shot of Babri Masjid.

Although the ensuing images may be read as a self-contained sequence, I wish to assign them to Shaila's point of view by drawing attention to her glance at the off-screen space, a look that previously seized the fearful image of militant Hindus. If we gloss over Shaila's place in the circuit of images in the unravelling riot sequences following the re-enacted scenes of demoliton, we can see how the film presents the Muslim inhabitants of Bombay, easily identifiable by their skull caps, as aggressors rather than as victims of taunting. However, if we attend to the logic of point-of-view shots, we can see how, in both instances, the film represents Hindu fundamentalism as a horrifying image that haunts the public spaces in Bombay and, by extension, the national imaginary.

If we dwell exclusively on the open images and off-screen spaces, a certain kind of cinematic language emerges, a language that signals movement through the device of cuts, tying disparate spaces into narrative temporality – the language of classical cinema, no less. Such a reading

டிசம்பர் 6, 1992 - அயோத்தி

Shaila Banu recalls Babri Masjid before it was razed by Hindu fundamentalists overlooks the film's preoccupation with ceaseless movement: trains speeding across the bridge; boats ferrying people; Shaila running to meet Shekhar and fleeing from him; Shekhar and Shaila's escape from the small town; dolly shots that encircle the singer at the wedding as well as our lovers at the fort, and so on. While *Bombay* offers us tremendous scope to absorb movement in the *mise en scène* and between frames, it would not be an exaggeration to state that the film is a textbook study of the mobility of the camera, particularly the Steadicam and its willing partner in crime, the hand-held camera. As the camera snakes behind Shaila Banu in a narrow tunnel during her furtive rendezvous with Shekhar, as it launches a series of swish pans to imitate Shekhar's longing at Bekal fort, or when it inhabits the point of view of the frightened twins as they are being doused with gasoline, we are privy to the malleability of time and space inaugurated by Garrett Brown in *Bound for Glory* (1975).[64] In a fascinating account of the invention and use of the Steadicam camera, Serena Ferrara reveals that it was initially conceived as a stunt camera by inaugurating a perceptual revolution, a fact also noted by film historian Jean-Pierre Geuens, who is sure F. W. Murnau would have approved of its agility.[65] Smoother than the hand-held camera, the Steadicam promises to abduct us and take us to spaces that early film-makers could only dream of: the cut surrenders to long takes.

Brown's invention did not go unnoticed by Indian film-makers, who were enthralled by the tremendous mobility afforded by the Steadicam in Stanley Kubrick's *The Shining* (1980), better known than *Bound for Glory*. However, there is substantial disagreement on who was the first film-maker to deploy the Steadicam in Indian films. L. V. Prasad of Prasad Productions imported a model and inaugurated the instrument by hosting a promotional in March 1984. According to the trade paper *Screen*, a four-minute shot was filmed without a cut at the first demonstration:

Steadicam followed the actors (L. V. Prasad, Chitra Sharma and three others) ascending and descending the staircases, moved rapidly across the split-level set and in between furniture and other props. In effect Steadicam substituted for dolly, crane and hand-held models. A second unit camera recorded all of this.[66]

The inauguration of the Steadicam in India in 1984. From left to right: documentary film-maker Navroze Contractor strapped with a Steadicam 2, head of Prasad Productions L. V. Prasad, an unidentified person and director Chetan Shah

The Steadicam in *Bombay*. From left to right: Steadicam operator Prasad, producer S. Sriram, art director Thotta Tharani, associate director U. V. Pani and director Mani Ratnam

The Steadicam was operated on this occasion by the documentary film-maker Navroze Contractor, a graduate of the Film and Television Institute of India (FTII), who was reportedly trained by Garrett Brown. Prasad recruited film director Chetan Shah, also present at the initial demonstration, to direct a short promotional film on the Steadicam. Shah submitted a treatment, but the film was never made.[67]

A competing version emerges from Hyderabad. Ramgopal Varma, the bad boy of Indian cinema, was making his first film, *Shiva* (1989). Enthralled by the fluidity of the Steadicam in *The Shining*, Varma was keen to deploy it in his film. After making enquiries, he found a Steadicam lying fallow at Prasad, unused for five years. The Steadicam was shipped to Hyderabad and used extensively in *Shiva*: a panting camera moves through college corridors, sneaks up stairs and stalks rogues.[68] The kinetic energy we detect and enjoy in Varma's films was undoubtedly fuelled by his early experiments with the Steadicam; *Shiva* is the first completed Indian film in which the Steadicam was used.

Another tale complicating its use in India is also available, a version that directly bears on the filming of *Bombay* and has its roots in Rajiv Menon's training as a cinematographer. According to Menon, his association with the Steadicam began in his final year at the Madras Film Institute, when each of the graduates is expected to produce a short written thesis in addition to a film.[69]He was working as an assistant to film-maker K. Hariharan on a documentary on the Tamil film star T. N. Krishnan. According to Menon:

The Steadicam was brought to location. The designated operator, Marcus Bartley Junior, said the monitor was not working, and he had a bad back, so I volunteered to shoot with the Steadicam with no monitor: it was like shooting blind handheld. Surprise, surprise, the shot had some useful moments. Mr Ramesh Prasad, head of Prasad Studios, hears of the incident and asks whether I could work and implement the dysfunctional Steadicam. I wrote a detailed report on the failure of the Steadicam and submitted the same to the Institute as my thesis. The report lay on Prasad's desk for a couple of months till Peter Waldeck, the then marketing head of Cinema

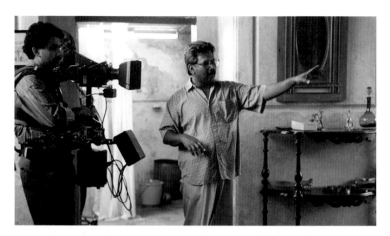

Products, was coming from Australia and stopped over in Madras to sell a
few more Steadicams in India. Mr Ramesh Prasad turned his offer down,
adding that a boy had written a report on the failure of the system – the
circuitry drive was tropicalised. Mr Waldeck said most of these problems are
fixed in the Steadicam 3 and, if Prasad sent this boy to the United States
they would train him and trade in your Steadicam 2 for the brand new
Steadicam 3. So I went to Silver Cup Studios in Queens, New York, to train
under the inventor of the system, Mr Garrett Brown.[70]

Prasad Productions has long been at the forefront of film technology in
India, as the standard-bearer for colour processing, sound mixing and
other technologies. It should come as no surprise that Prasad wished to
have well-trained Steadicam operators and sponsored Menon's training in
the United States. On his return from the US, Menon started his career as
a migrant cinematographer for Prasad Videos. Armed with a Steadicam 3,
he moved from one film set to another for as little as Rs 200 per film.
Filming inane chase sequences tired him out, and he gave up a career in
cinema for advertising, until *Bombay*.

   Indisputably, the Steadicam was handy in the re-creation of a war-torn
city, but it also quickly became adept in shooting the more intimate scenes.
Nowhere else is its agility more apparent than in a poignant moment

Mani Ratnam directing Steadicam operator Rajiv Menon in *Bombay* between Shekhar and Shaila. Before we get to the tango performed by the Steadicam, let us retrace our steps leading up to this moment. Shekhar's presence at the wedding assures him of Shaila's interest in the 'Kannalane' song-and dance-sequence, but her name eludes him. Where else would he go but to the wharf to wait for the group of *burqa*-clad women and a chance breeze to catch a glimpse of Shaila? Refusing to heed doomsday predictions from his friend that include beatings and a summons from the Panchayat, Shekhar stares hard at the approaching band of *burqas*: the Steadicam simulates his search by scanning from right to left. Not only does Shaila straggle, but the temperamental breeze lifts her veil, and the Steadicam swiftly inspects her face and spots the red bag – her distinguishing mark in a sea of black.

What follows is a comedy of mistaken identities as Shekhar waits at the wharf; a running train and dissolve mark the passage of time. Shaila dupes Shekhar by exchanging bags with her friend, who is reduced to tears

The Steadicam simulates Shekhar's search for Shaila by scanning the crowd and finding her red bag

by Shekhar's advances and inadvertently blurts out Shaila's name. Shekhar is ecstatic, yelling out her name as the two women run in slow motion and the streaming music underscores his passion. In addition to the breeze and the rain characterising the *mise en scène* of their desire, it slowly becomes clear that the Steadicam has been complicitous in advancing and slicing the space of action. The real tour de force, however, is just around the corner.

We move from the blue hues of the rain to a bright scene on a landing inside Shekhar's home that appears to serve as his bedroom. Shekhar seems to be tiptoeing around looking for a cigarette, which materialises from under a pillow, but the camera positioned at the head of the stairs is more interested in the scene below. It tilts down as if to eavesdrop: Shaila has dropped in to borrow Lakshmi's notes from the chemistry class. We have to wonder if her interest in alchemy is a ruse to visit Shekhar or an unconscious concoction of her desire? Lakshmi exits the frame to fetch her notes, but the camera lingers to watch Shaila fiddle self-consciously. From the off-screen space, we hear Shekhar calling out to his sister. Shaila is startled, but it is only on his second bellow that she responds: 'Lakshmi has gone in.' The camera yields to a quick crane to reach Shekhar on the landing. This long take unravels into a series of shot-reverse-shots that, taking advantage of the narrow stairwell, rotate in the tight space, mimicking Shekhar and Shaila's yearning. Lakshmi's re-entry breaks their interlocking looks, and, as Shaila flees in embarrassment, Shekhar yells her name from the balcony. She turns to meet his look and then repositions her veil, rushing homeward.

By tying a tilt and a crane in one movement, the film weds Shekhar to Shaila, replacing for ever an older language of desire so lovingly analysed by Raymond Bellour in his analysis of twelve shots in *The Big Sleep* (1946) – twelve shots to have the macho film noir detective Phillip Marlowe utter 'I guess I'm in love with you,' over an image of Vivian Rutledge's face. That rhythm of splicing to express seems to have made a quiet exit in *Bombay*. In one fell swoop, the camera moves between two spaces, rendering their partition irrelevant, insisting that it is a flimsy excuse to keep the lovers apart; their social differences appear equally superfluous.

The agility of the Steadicam in a narrow stairwell

Even the narrow stairwell invites the camera to squeeze in and rotate, to grab reaction shots that will subsequently be spliced together as shot-reverse-shots. It is almost impossible not to be snared by the camera – the human figures seem so inconsequential in this dance.

Given the dexterity of the Steadicam, it is not surprising to see it being deployed in the sequences of collective violence besieging the city, travelling above crowds or slipping between alleyways. The riot sequences unfolding before the interval dovetail the demolition of Babri Masjid, commencing after a fade to white: a group of men with swords and sticks, whose skullcaps clearly identify them as Muslims, charges through the narrow streets of Bombay. A police van arrives but is assaulted by the crowd and later burned; shops are looted; vegetable carts are toppled; and the twins Kamal and Kabir are caught in crossfire. A vendor's cart set on fire works as an effective cover for rioters tossing Molotov cocktails at the police. The camera is mobile only a couple of times, most prominently as it stalks along a balcony – probably a fragment of a censored scene in which a woman tumbles over the balcony after being hit by a stray bullet fired by the police. Once the police start shooting into the mob, we see, in rapid succession, random bodies succumbing to bullets that pierce their backs as they attempt to flee to safety. Shaila and Shekhar just manage to save their sons from being immolated by a group of hooded men. It is here that the Steadicam simulates the point of view of the twins. The family huddles together protecting itself from police fire. The family-planning slogan 'We

The interval in *Bombay* is declared (in Tamil) following the Steadicam riot sequences

two, our two' is plastered on a nearby wall adding an ironic touch, and the film breaks for an interval.

By having the police arrive well after the urban space has been taken over by violence and deliberately fire into a receding populace casts them as brutal and communalised – a representation that is widely accepted in the public sphere.[71] All too frequently in the film, figures of the state – police and the paramilitary – either arrive too late, cause a stampede that separates the twins or disappear during the long sequences of violence; considered together, their delay relays the film's ideological investment in seeking a resolution for communal harmony outside the purview of the state. This disappointment with the state and the desire to curtail its role is a recurring theme in Ratnam's films: vigilante resolutions in *Nayakan* and *Thalapathi/The Chief* (1991); heroism diminishing military power in *Roja*; suicide bombing circumventing the symbolic power of the state in *Dil Se*, and so on. However, the irony is not lost on us that *Bombay* was tweaked and trimmed by the state Board of Censors, with ample intrusion from politicians like Bal Thackeray. Even if the police delayed controlling the violence that erupted in the streets of Bombay, the Board of Censors seems to be standing in the wings whispering instructions on the direction of the narrative. It is not that the state has scored a quiet victory but that any reading of the film will have to view the narrative resolutions as brushing against the demands of the censors, a tussle that governs both the production of the film and our viewing of it.[72]

The searing closure before the interval did not go unnoticed by Rajiv Menon. Mortified by the narrow escape suffered by the family, Menon remembers telling Ratnam that if he was intent on showing such extreme scenes of violence before the interval, what could possibly exceed such cruelty in the second half? Ratnam did not retreat from his script and responded that he wanted the audience to be transfixed as they filed out for the break, gasping and wondering what surprises awaited them once the film resumed. The audience was not let down.

The second half of the film is a narrative of irreparable loss amplified by a sadistic, punitive impulse. For instance, after a long absence from the diegesis, Shekhar's father and Shaila's parents suddenly appear at their children's apartment concerned about their welfare, but this image of an united extended family is an ephemeral one: the family is drawn into the outburst of violence that rocked Bombay on 5 January, 1993, a month after Babri Masjid was levelled by Hindu fundamentalists. As communities rage against each other, the family is thrown asunder: all the parents are killed and the twins are initially separated from their parents and, later, from each other.

A landscape of ruin awaits us once the film resumes: a naked infant wanders through the burning remnants of a riot; a wailing woman, pregnant with hopelessness, is stranded. A camera meanders through this landscape, finally reaching Shekhar, who shares the despondency expressed on the soundtrack. As the sections unfold after the interval, the film fails to recover the utopian hopes that propelled Shaila and Shekhar to Bombay, projecting instead an unending series of catastrophes reminiscent of the more punitive

Scenes of death and violence post-interval

aspects of horror films that overlap easily with the film genre classified by Vasudevan as 'cinema of urban anxiety' that 'conveys to us the exhilaration of the dread'.[73] A barrage of images fills the screen: the crowds in the first half of the film signifying urban collectivities morph into mobs running amok through the streets of the city; the faithful at both mosque and temple wait vigilantly for the next order to rampage; anxious lines of relatives look for family members at the police station; and rows of brutalised corpses at the morgue are presented for our inspection.

Narrating the violent transformation in the urban fabric, the film text undergoes a significant shift by drawing us into the *mise en scène* of horror, most notably by increasing the mobility of the Steadicam. Unlike the first half of the movie, in which the Steadicam heightens our relationship with erotic desire by perching us like nosy voyeurs in the most intimate scenes, it becomes a menacing force in the second half. Curving down the hallways of a government building, the Steadicam keeps us focused on the questions Shekhar poses to a senior police officer about Muslims being primary targets of police fire in the violence that erupted after 6 December. On other occasions, the camera acquires feline qualities as it wanders through spaces of the Shakti Samaj office and sneaks beside Shekhar as he interviews the chief about provoking his cadres. Swish pans rush us from the Shakti Samaj offices to the office of a leader of the Muslim community.

The camera's ceaseless, restless travel through different spaces simulates neurasthenia, additionally heightening the impression of a ravaged urban space decimated by violence. However, the most evocative deployment of the Steadicam comes in the recording of two of the many violent events, which included pogroms, police shootings and bomb blasts, that wreaked havoc on the city between January and March 1993. The first of these, unfolds immediately after the 'Kuchi Kuchi Rakamma' song-and-dance sequence. It is late at night and a subtitle running across the frame marks the date as 5 January, 1993, a month after the first riots of 6 December. A roving Steadicam enters a warehouse and probes the cavernous spaces emptied of humanity before rushing into an alley lined with trucks. Hiding behind a truck, the camera focuses on a man

The Steadicam stalks a worker through an alley; he is found dead the next day

stumbling towards a wall to urinate. The stalking camera assaults him. All he can muster is a petrified look at the surprise attack – a shot that we have seen in countless horror films, from *Peeping Tom* (1960) to *Scream* (1996). The film cuts to a high angle-shot and it is daylight. We see a group rushing to the scene of the accident, where two dead bodies are offered for our scrutiny, representing a rallying cause demanding vengeance and counterattacks. On the soundtrack, the voice of a newscaster lends indexical signification – two *mathadi*s (the labouring class) have been killed in Dongri – and is further bolstered by shots of Shekhar at the printing press lifting a freshly minted newspaper that declares in bold letters: 'BOMBAY BURNS'.[74]

Tension reigns in the city as the film cuts to Shaila's father, Basheer, at the mosque with one of the twins. The next cut takes us to a rally at a temple – a *maha aarati* – where we spot Shekhar's father, Narayana Pillai, and the other twin. As Pillai walks home with his grandson, he is confronted by a sword-wielding group of Muslims. Basheer suddenly appears and rescues him by claiming Pillai as one of his own. Gingerly squeezed between segments depicting volatile communal tensions among Hindus and Muslims, the scene of appeasement between the warring fathers is long overdue. But their peace is short-lived. The wandering Steadicam strikes again, this time edited in slow motion or, according to Menon, in a step-freeze editing process.[75]

Once again, in the middle of the night, the Steadicam travels through an alley until it reaches a shanty and halts at the swastika on the door. A human arm enters the frame and locks the door, while another figure throws a pail of gasoline over it. The scene inside is choked with disaster: a handicapped girl struggles to rise from her wheelchair and a distressed family realises its fatal predicament. Within seconds, their home goes up in flames, letting loose a fevered chaos into the urban space as day breaks.[76] Shekhar and Shaila are part of a crowd fleeing from the marauding streets to the safety of their home, which is soon revealed to be a bad idea. From this point on, the film never lets up, leading us from one scene of chaos and tragedy to another, with family members torn apart as the city goes up in flames.

As in the riots that followed the demolition of Babri Masjid, *Bombay* recalls events that fuelled the violent incidents in the early months of 1993. But there is a significant difference between its representation of the events in December and those in January. As we have seen in the sequences following the levelling of Babri Masjid, the film exploits the mobility of the Steadicam to convey the density of urban spaces, but it adopts the point of view of the omniscient narrator. In contrast, when narrating the events in January, the film reels us into the visual economy. Replacing the omniscient narrator, the camera preys, stalks and assaults innocent victims in similarly mobile scenes in *The Shining* and *Evil Dead 2* (1987). Lacking the comfort and distance of the omniscient narrator, these sequences draw us into the diegesis by not only aligning us with the camera but also by stripping away the possibility of a protagonist as our proxy; in short, we become the aggressors.

In both these violent incidents initiated by the Steadicam, Hindus are the victims. In the second case, the camera, arriving at the Hindu home, isolates Muslims as arsonists. However, another logic overrides the choice of Muslims as aggressors – the logic of keeping scores that carefully tabulates a list of attacks and grievances. It is the working of this dreadful bookkeeping that leads us to a scene in which a taxi carrying a Muslim family is waylaid by a Hindu mob. Trapping the Muslim family inside the locked taxi that is set on fire by the mob, the camera conveys the passengers' and its own delirium.

By activating the camera's role in these violent incidents, the film

Narayanan Pillai is struck by the camera

raises a range of questions that plague the ethics of reporting, narrating and re-enacting vicious incidents in the social and political imaginary. The breadth of visual and written material on the events that took place between December 1992 and March 1993, with which Ratnam seems familiar, is impressive in its detail. However, what the film offers is a reconsideration of the relationships between the cinematic eye and political events. As we have seen, the film's narration of the violence erupting in the streets of Bombay after the demolition of Babri Masjid initially assumes the non-sectarian version. This happens despite excisions recommended by the Board of Censors and the film's gaps in causality: the police arrive well after the eruption of violence and do not hesitate to fire into the crowd, fatally wounding several. After the interval, however, the film strikes a different note: instead of merely re-enacting events, it foregrounds the cinematic writing of such events, including our fascination with their unfolding – who did what to whom, when did the police arrive, and so on. By emphasising the camera's connivance in these events, the film suggests that our perception of them cannot be divorced from the way in which they are arranged and presented to us, even if we have to borrow from the grammar of genre films. What is exposed in these two instances is the underbelly of our presumed concern, our fascination with the minutiae of violence as well as with cinematic images.

Lest we assume that the film underplays the role of the family and reserves its pointed critique of political events for the second half of the film, I want to draw attention to the camera's viciousness towards the parents. While Shekhar, Shaila and their children manage to escape their bombed apartment, the visiting parents scramble awkwardly to get out: Narayana Pillai interrupts Basheer's prayers – is this Nero fiddling while Rome burns? When Basheer goes back to the burning room to retrieve his Koran, Pillai stops him but then returns to the room to rescue the holy book; the cooking gas cylinder slowly attracts the surrounding flames and finally combusts, drawing Basheer and his wife into the inferno. We see a long shot of the apartment going up in flames. But all is not over. A swirl of light moves in the direction of Pillai, who clutches the Koran; the camera and bright lights meant to startle the actor finally strike him in a swift swish pan. His bigotry is knocked down by the camera, which seems unimpressed by this belated evidence of his tolerance.

Similarly, despite the profusion of indexical signification, following the interval, the film exploits the Steadicam's playfulness, recalling the use of the Hitchcockian Mcguffin in horror films. An eerie calm settles on the city as paramilitary forces patrol the streets. In the distance, we see the eunuch, who rescued Kamal from a stampede, quietly escorting him through the streets. The Steadicam, watching them from a narrow lane that lends the scene a menacing feel, is undeterred by a passing military van but stops short of assaulting the eunuch and Kamal, an action that, by now, we expect of the camera. We are reeled into a structure of anticipation common to horror films that keeps us on the edge of our seats, waiting for the next strike. We are a far cry from concerned citizen-subjects seeking a cessation of violence.

Open images, off-screen spaces and the restless camera – both hand-held and the Steadicam – in *Bombay* induce the spectre of the 'other' and mobilise the structure of anticipation that we associate with horror films. However, such a reading of genre-specific features, available globally, overlooks cinematic convention particular to the composition of popular cinema. The structure of suspense has long been available to audiences of popular Indian cinema, particularly in connection with the knockout song-and-dance numbers. However jaded we are to the temporal unspooling of a popular film, the exact timing of these interruptions carries an element of surprise, provoking loud gasps or thunderous claps from the audience. Typically, music streams from an off-screen space, a moment of non-action is transformed into a vigorous song-and-dance number, and the dizzying movement of the camera opens up new spaces of action and reconfigures spatial and temporal continuity.

For the outsider, the colour-laden song-and-dance sequences are the most enticing feature of Indian popular cinema: *Ghost World* (2000) opens with a jittery twist to signify our angst-ridden heroine's secret pleasures; *My Family's Honor* (1997) cuts to a cheery number to alleviate the desires of Algerian migrants in France; and Baz Luhrmann has openly admitted that *Moulin Rouge* (2001) emulates Bollywood musicals. Before we tackle the viability of employing the term 'musical' to describe this popular cinema, it is worth returning to *Indian Cinema*, Barnouw and Krishnaswamy's mammoth undertaking, which informs us that Indian talkies always had songs: the first sound feature, Ardeshir Irani's *Alam Ara/Beauty of the World* (1931), has over seven songs; another early Hindi film had forty songs, and, not to be outdone, a Tamil film had sixty.[77] Film historians and musicologists suggest that the popularity and persistence of songs point to Indian cinema's early links to conventions of nineteenth-century Parsi theatre and folk theatre, which were, similarly, scenes strung together with songs.[78]

Although musicologists have written extensively on the synthetic quality of Indian film songs and on the parallel economy of star music directors and singers, there is an absence of literature on song picturisation, reinforcing the popular assumption that the sequences are extra-diegetic. It is difficult not to consider the quick cut to Switzerland or Australia in a film as an attraction whose sole purpose seems to be relief from the summer heat for the film-makers, a tourist excursion that reminds us of cinema's promise of virtual travel as early as the Lumière shorts. A perusal of contemporary films in India reveals a tourist map with destinations to such cities as London, Sydney and New York; photogenic locales of New Zealand and Switzerland; and the pristine beaches of South Africa and Seychelles. Domestic landscapes include historical monuments and, most recently, an eager return to Kashmir valley.

Once a film cuts to an exotic locale, we often find our protagonists gyrating to music with calisthenic vigour reminiscent of the Rocketts, accompanied by a group of dancers. Since the 1980s, the restrained gestures of lovelorn actors or the seductive dance of the vamp has had to bow to the choreographer's bidding whose vision is of a troupe of dancers who can perform calibrated moves to throbbing music. It is impossible to find a box-office success without the input of star choreographers, such as Saroj Khan, Farah Khan, Prabhu Deva and several others whose names in the opening credits vie with the music director, art director and cinematographer. Ratnam has extensively used choreographers in his films, including the current rage Farah Khan; for *Bombay*, he recruited Prabhu Deva and Raju Sundaram for three spectacular dance numbers.

Mindful that the success of a popular film depends on the music, Ratnam has actively upheld the role of the music director from the beginning – for example, star musician Ilyaraja was a key draw in his early Tamil films. However, it is his collaboration with A. R. Rahman since *Roja* that has won him acclaim from national and international audiences. Rahman has emerged as a boy wonder, orchestrating music for Hindi and Tamil films with occasional forays into the diaspora. More recently, he collaborated with Andrew Lloyd Webber in the musical *Bollywood Dreams*. A casual surfing of television channels in India also highlights his success as a composer of advertisement jingles, his signature most legible in spirited nationalist tunes set against national icons, both human and architectural.

Admittedly, despite the availability of world class musicians in India, the task of filming these song-and-dance sequences and connecting them to a taut narrative with generic impulses can be trying. Film-makers keen on experimenting with narrative have often dispensed with such sequences altogether, seeing them as as pure distraction: in *Munna/Lost Child* (1954), a social realist film, K. A. Abbas thought it inappropriate to include such sequences in a searing narrative of poverty; the Tamil film *Antha Nal/That Day* (1954) similarly stuck to a continuous narrative of pain without song-and-dance numbers; B. R. Chopra chose the format of a thriller when he excised the song-and-dance sequences in *Ittefaq* (1969); P. C. Sriram abandoned them in his political thriller *Kurudhippunal/River of Blood* (1995); Ram Gopal Varma refused to include songs in his horror films *Kaun/Who?* (1998) and *Bhooth/Ghost* (2003), even as delaying devices. Besides challenging distributors, who often insist on including these marketable segments, these experiments assume that song-and-dance sequences are oddities in action films and a natural fit in melodrama and love stories. At the same time, however, any consideration of auteurism in Indian popular cinema must contend with a director's ability to incorporate song-and-dance numbers effectively into a film, notwithstanding a film's preoccupation with genre features.

In this regard, an evaluation of Ratnam's films reveals his ability to commandeer the various elements of popular cinema, constantly fine-tuning its look and pace in a way that reveals his engagement with global genres, whether a gangster film such as *Nayakan* or *Thalapathi*, marriage stories in *Mouna Ragam* and *Alaipayuthey*, or topicals in *Roja*, *Bombay* and *Dil Se*. Despite the virtuosity of his film-making style and the range of his repertoire, Ratnam admits to finding song-and-dance sequences an uphill battle. A feeling of relief, he claims, washes over him each time he finishes shooting one of these extravagant numbers.[79] Despite his own sense of being hemmed in, a reading of Ratnam's films points to his wide range of experiments with this convention.

I have proposed elsewhere in my reading of *Nayakan* that at least five types of spatial and temporal links to the narrative obtain in his films, including their use as delaying devices, metaphors or metonymies.[80]

As in Ratnam's other films, the different categories in *Bombay* undergo substantial revision as they are adapted to the demands of the genre. Advertised and read as a love story, *Bombay* had the requisite number of songs, but this reading revises received wisdom twice over: first, it identifies the narrative as belonging squarely within the genre of a marriage story, as honed by Ratnam, and second, it incorporates elements of the horror genre. Hybrid genres are not uncommon in popular cinema, which often uses the interval as a decisive punctuation mark to graft together two different genres. The trade papers seem to see *Bombay* in precisely those terms: a first half of relative calm and a second half of mayhem. Even a quick look at the film will dispel such facile divisions. The film complicates the welding of genres by smuggling in aspects of horror films early on, most prominently in the song-and-dance sequences. In proposing such a reading, I do not wish to lose sight of the fact that these sequences exploit the decorative and gendered attractiveness that routinely inflects them: Koirala blossoms in these sequences, undercutting her otherwise meek presence in the film.

At times – for instance, in his gangster films *Nayakan* and *Thalapathi* and in *Alaipayuthey* – Ratnam ties the credit sequence to a background score that emerges as the leitmotif in the film. In *Bombay*, however, he delays the arrival of a song-and-dance sequence until well after Shekhar and Shaila have spotted each other at the pier. From the rain-drenched scenes at the pier, we cut to a sunny day at a Muslim wedding, to which a reluctant Shekhar accompanies his sister. The motif of chance encounters governs when Shekhar spots Shaila giggling amid a gaggle of girls. The song sets up a hide-and-seek game; the ornate structure of Tirumala Nayak palace showcases a hybrid architectural style, providing the perfect *mise en scène* for the intercommunal couple. There are no references in the film to distant travel from Maanguddi in Nellai District to the wedding scene, but we know that a cut has ushered us from monsoon-hit Kasargod to sunny Madurai. In the hands of a lesser film-maker, such a spatial disruption would be pure attraction, a lame excuse to travel outdoors. But, in *Bombay*, the choice of the architectural space and its definite links to the narrative undercut such explanations. Shaila dominates the 'Kannalane' song, which affirms her desire and seduces Shekhar. With the wedding party in the margins serving as an audience, this sequence bears a close resemblance to the backstage musical that Ratnam has extensively used in his other films.

Visual motifs in the 'Kannalane' sequence overlap with the narrative, transforming it from a dull to a vigorous realisation that follows the specific preoccupations of this narrative. The curtains, dupattas and filigreed screens recall Shaila's veil, staging, as Ravi Vasudevan suggests, the *mise en abyme* of the film that recurs again later. The circular dolly moving around the singer in the courtyard underscores the film's obsession with movement, and, finally, the ghostly 'open' image closes the song, intruding into the seduction scene, emphasising the film's dual erotics: love and violence.

While a cut mobilises virtual travel in the first song-and-dance sequence, the frenetic energy of an intercutting segment moves the song picturisation of 'Uyire/My Soul', in which both architecture and clothing emerge as metaphors in the topography of desire.[81] A freely dangling camera simulates Shekhar's tumultuous desire as he waits for Shaila at Bekal fort; a stormy sea and grey skies heighten his desolation. The film cuts to another space and we find that Shaila, having sneaked away from

Production stills showing the 'Kallananae' song being directed by Mani Ratnam

the bustle at home, hurries to the wharf with a friend. A boat delivers her to the fort, but Shekhar seems unaware of her efforts, cutting himself with a handy knife to express his possessed desire for her. Shaila responds to his singing with her own verses, assuring us that locked gates will not stop her from keeping her date. We are relieved when Shekhar spots her in the distance, framed by the scalloped turrets of the castle wall. But, as if to hold her back, yet another hurdle blocks their union as her *burqa* snags on the tip of an anchor; keeping pace with the transgressions depicted in the film, Shaila slips out of her black robe and runs towards Shekhar. A hypnotised dolly circles the embracing couple, unable to stop till the end of the song, when Shaila, as if on cue from the paternal scene of law, untangles herself from the embrace and rushes out of the scene of desire. Shekhar is left to weather the storm as the sequence ends in a strange way, after having celebrated the couple's desire to unite despite transgressions. This closure is, however, in sync with the film's covert consorting with the horror genre, in which it is not surprising to find mesmerised protagonists left to their own devices in abandoned forts or castles.

Menon considers 'Uyire' one of Rahman's best love ballads, and regards the picturisation as 'pure and simple'. With *Bombay* scheduled during the monsoons, heavy rains drenched film-making for the first couple of days, continuing to threaten shooting with regular downpours. Menon had visited the Bekal fort for personal reasons – his interest in maritime history and in his father's career as a naval officer – long before this assignment. Once the film was under way, he was haunted by that imposing structure, as was Ratnam, who did not need to be convinced to use its stoic splendour. The simplicity of composition happened partly by accident, partly by design. Only one camera, with its filters off, was employed for the shoot; it craned above Shekhar and stalked Shaila through a tunnel in the fort. Koirala's blue dress, which accentuated the blue and black hues of the film, was pure caprice: she was meant to wear a pink dress, but the wardrobe person misplaced it, happening to retrieve a blue one from the clothes rack assigned for the 'Kannalane' dance. The air was heavy with moisture, the camera filters were off and the abandoned British fort undoubtedly evoked English meadows, an image that Menon

The 'Uyire' song: the couple are united after Shaila slips out of her burka

returned to later in a picturisation of a song in his own film *Kandukondain Kandukondain*, for which he travelled to Scotland. The melodrama of the song 'Uyire' hitting a crescendo overshadows the continuity gaffes that Menon points out – the close-up shot of Shaila without her *burqa* before the dramatic moment in which she throws it off, or the flamboyant way in which she crosses the 180-degree space of action.

In contrast to the haunting separation that closes the sequences in which 'Kannalane' and 'Uyire' are sung, a sliver of a song sung in a gusty Marathi voice rejoicing Shaila and Shekhar's marriage plays on the soundtrack in a later scene as they run out of the registrar's office in Bombay and board a city bus. The song almost seems truncated from a longer number that may have covered the couple's spatial journey to their home, a device that Ratnam used most effectively in the opening sequences in *Nayakan* and *Thalapathy*, in which cinematic geography trumps over spatial disruptions. The wisp of a song rushes our couple through the city towards their home, as if to underplay the celebratory aspects of their wedding. The film delays this celebration till Remo Fernandez belts out 'Humma Humma' on the soundtrack, and Prabhu Deva and Sonali Bendre swing to his beat with a chorus of dancers in what the industry refers to as an item number – an extravagant song-and-dance routine led by a prominent model or star – whose explicit purpose is to showcase a choreographer's talent or a star's relationship to the production outfit. Often extra-diegetic in popular cinema, such item

The newly-married Shekhar and Shaila walk along Marine Brive, Bombay

numbers are, in Ratnam's films, pulled into the narrative, tempering our desire to walk out of the theatre or, if we are at home, to press the fast-forward buttons of our remotes.

'Humma Humma' begins after Shekhar playfully greets the prostitutes in his neighbourhood and walks home with Shaila. The couple is welcomed by the departure of a group of rambunctious kids who had taken over their home. Relieved to have their privacy, Shekhar and Shaila gingerly embrace, but the film cuts to a brothel where a dance number has begun, preferring its energy, and yet, it returns at intervals to Shekhar and Shaila's lovemaking. Instead of serving as a pure metaphor in which the two spaces – Shekhar and Shaila's bedroom and the brothel – have no diegetic relationship, the film connects them explicitly by directing us to see Shekhar looking at the dancers in the brothel and the newlywed couple mimicking their movements. Graphic matches supplied by veils and entangled bodies further entwine the two spaces, even as they are distinguished by different speeds of action – slow-motion shots of dancers inform the couple's lingering passion in the bedroom. In the final moments of the sequence, the film abandons the cloistered bedroom to veer off into the courtyard, where the dancers' movements take on metaphoric meaning through a fire blazing in the background. The blaze underlines Shekhar and Shaila's passion, which, because of censorship, cannot be shown.

There is no doubt that Ratnam deftly uses the spectacular aspects of the song-and-dance interruption to circumvent the prohibitions laid down by censorship whose limits he was tempted to test in *Roja*, the 'Rukmini!Rukmini!' number provoked the Board of Censors. Although censorship is the dominant factor to reckon with when reading this number in *Bombay*, it is worth considering Vasudevan's proposition that the intercutting of the two scenes introduces another level of prohibition in popular cinema – the cinematic representation of a sexual union between a Muslim and a Hindu. What Vasudevan implies is that this prohibition exceeds censorship dictates, as if such a union is too horrifying to represent on screen.[82]

The 'Humma Humma' song and dance routine

As the film unfolds, the song-and-dance sequences stage the anxieties of an intercommunal union in the midst of social and political antagonisms, even in an upbeat number such as 'Halla Gulla'. Passion in one number leads to pregnancy in another. Tapping into the possibilities of temporal discontinuity in this convention, 'Halla Gulla' effortlessly scrambles the scenes of marriage and stages of pregnancy: a fully pregnant Shaila emerges as a young bride. Temporal discontinuities also lead to utopian unions between two communities: Shekhar dons a skullcap on one outing, and Shaila surreptitiously smears a *bindi* on her forehead. Charged with possibilities, the song breaks, and the film recalls the squabbling fathers in Maanguddi; Narayana Pillai visits Basheer with news of Shaila's pregnancy, but their belligerency leads to petty squabbling, signalling the beginnings of a comedy track. The film cuts to a gliding Steadicam in a hospital corridor, where strands of music cannot completely ease Shaila's pain and fear. The sequence is augmented by shots of dark spaces and clunky elevators. We cannot help but see the hospital as a terrifying *mise en scène* found in the subgenre of medical-horror films: plastic surgery, comatose patients, the birth of monstrous twins, and so on. The second part of the song adopts a linear trajectory as it charts the birth and growth of the twins against the backdrop of iconic landmarks in Bombay.

The constructed geography of the film allows us to travel smoothly with the cut from the Gateway of India to the studio set in the Campa Cola estates. Effectively, the sequence collapses large-scale temporal shifts into one number – a style that is also evident in *Nayakan*'s 'Ne Uru Kadal Sangeetham/You Are a Love Song.' In *Bombay*, the 'Halla Gulla' sequence reveals the film's kinship with the horror genre by dividing the number into two parts, drawing attention to the precarious state of the intercommunal family during the period in which Hindu fundamentalism was on the rise. Scenes of pregnancy and marriage do not lead directly to the birth of twins without a detour to Maanguddi, and the end of the song is signalled by a knock at the door and the arrival of the militant Hindu Shakit Samaj cadres.

After the interval, the song-and-dance sequences emulate the shift in narrative as the film lurches towards recounting the inflamed communal

The 'Hulla Gulla' songs charts Shaila's pregnancy, the birth of her twin sons at the hospital, and the twins' childhood amid the iconic landmarks of Bombay

tensions in Bombay. Shaila's parents and Shekhar's father arrive in Bombay after the destruction of Babri Masjid in December 1992, when the city was besieged with violence. Their attempts at rapprochement with their children are met with little protest, but the grandfathers continue to quarrel over the religious identities of their grandsons. On one occasion, when the grandfathers are plotting to take the grandchildren to the village, the scene quickly regresses into a squabble that causes the twins to hide in their parents' bedroom. Shekhar jokingly says that it seems like a fine idea to send the boys to stay with their grandparents, suggesting that he and Shaila perhaps can parent a little girl. Shaila coquettishly declines his offer, a reaction that permits the film to cut suddenly to a lush, hilly landscape.

Dressed as a gypsy, Shaila leads a chorus of young girls who refuse the advances of a group of men led by Shekhar and their sons. Shot in Ooty, the sylvan landscape in the song-and-dance sequence 'Kuchi Kuchi Rakamma/Little one' provides a respite from the communal and familial antagonisms in Bombay, but the jarring spatial disjunction underscores the convention's function as a device used to delay in a narrative increasingly shaped by a salacious interest in acts of violence. Instead of a round of violence bursting in on the cozy family, now reunited, the film grants privileges to an extra-diegetic outburst, with textual violence doubling as social and political violence. We watch in awe as the structure of anticipation particular to horror films confers its energy onto an extra-diegetic number, reminding us of the 'shock and awe' exuberance of a montage of attractions.

More often than not, extra-diegetic song-and-dance numbers in Indian popular cinema tend to be fairly benign, characterised by touristic impulses that overwhelm narrative relevance. However, as I have suggested elsewhere, these photogenic landscapes are not without ideological charge: scenes of Kashmir naturalise their place in an Indian nationalist cartography. Here, too, the random inclusion of a deforested Ooty, populated by gypsies, replaces the communal strife between Hindus and Muslims in Bombay. Tribal peoples and gypsies have had a stock presence in song-and-dance sequences in Indian popular cinema, metonymically extending associations of innocence to the narrative. This is

true of *Bombay*, where it appears that the sexual energies of the couple now have to be re-routed through Ooty, deforestation notwithstanding, when faced with the threat of communal riots.

The film turns decidedly punitive after this extra-diegetic excursion, unsparing at every register: parents die a violent death, twins are separated and the city faces another round of violence beginning in January 1993. Communities unleash violence against each other; wielding weapons, men rush through the streets possessed with an irrational rage. Visual images underscore communal identities; skullcaps and saffron bandanas, markers of religious identity, seem unreasonably definitive in the chaos of the urban space. Keen to record the entropy engulfing the city, in which the logic of cause and effect has gone awry or the deadly link between perpetrator and victim has been irreparably damaged, the film seizes the grammar of the song-and-dance sequence.

The roving camera orchestrates our relationship with this segment by tilting up a flight of stairs to watch a pair of *burqa*-clad women rush to join a group witnessing a violent altercation on the street. Drumbeats on the soundtrack coincide with a cut to the street as words in Hindi roll out 'Ruku jaao/Stop it' as the opening of a chant that later shifts to a song in Tamil that begs the crowds to cease this bloody violence. While the film maintains spatial continuity in this song, 'Idu Annai Bhoomi/This Mother Earth', the camera abandons temporal continuity as it zooms into a violent scene and cranes over rallies forming before Hindu and Muslim leaders; or takes us behind a filigreed wall hiding predators shooting into a group of unsuspecting

The 'Kuchi Kuchi Rakamma' song and dance sequence

The twins witness Hindu fundamentalists setting fire to a taxi carrying Muslim passengers

Muslim men fleeing one scene of torment only to be fatally wounded in another; or stalks the twins, who weave in and out of the mayhem and provide narrative continuity. Alternating between acts of violence instigated by Muslims and Hindus, the film suggests a certain equanimity that goaded critics, who reminded Ratnam that more Muslims than Hindus were victims of the violent acts in Bombay during this period and that there was no one Muslim leader to equal Thackeray's command in the city.

In the midst of the violence, the film cannot help presenting us with a familiar image found in the *mise en scène* of Ratnam's films: the automobile. Cars glide through his films, either hinting at temporal shifts in the narrative, precipitating a narrative or asserting their status as decoration. *Bombay*, however, prefers its cars burning. A police vehicle occupies centre stage as it is doused with kerosene in the middle of this segment, and, moments later, we watch the twins staring fixedly at a group of Hindus setting fire to a taxi and its terrified Muslim passengers; the Steadicam, if we recall, has managed to slip into the burning vehicle. Indexing the events of January 1993, the film competes with the director's imprint, each cinematic gesture jostling with and evoking different memories of the public space, simultaneously cinematic and political. The beat of the song 'Ruku Jaao' accentuates the commotion on screen; the sequence ends solemnly with the image of a blazing car, a lonely symbol of carnage that doubles as the figure of both mourning and ornamentation in Ratnam's cinema.

After an intermediary section detailing the arrival of paramilitary forces that rudely separate the twins, the eerie calm of a curfew saturates the ruined urban space. However, the paramilitary seems ineffectual and the city is besieged by another outburst of mayhem; on the soundtrack, a strand of 'Idu Annai Bhoomi' reminds us of a scorching connection between the acts of violence. Once again, an inflamed car and a blazing human body underscore the horrors of the aggression.

The recurring dissonance between the violence unfolding on screen and chants on the soundtrack to end the bloodshed eventually concludes with scenes of remorse: the Hindu leader drives through a desolate city and the Muslim leader collapses at the sight of bloodied bodies lying

The end of the violence: the knives are dropped and communities are reunited

across the narrow lanes of a neighbourhood. Despite our knowledge of Thackeray's claim that he felt no regret, or of the Board of Censors' recommendation that the voiceover expressing remorse be excised, we are relieved to see a turning point in the cycle of vengeance. Pleas to arrest the killings arise from the eunuch, who had not only saved Kamal earlier but had also stood up to a group of vengeful Hindu men; a Muslim woman embraces a Hindu woman as a sister, a symbolic gesture that mystifies her neighbours; and Shekhar holds centre stage as he reasons with the rioters to stop attacking each other.

In slow motion, we watch as saffron headbands are loosened, torches are thrown into puddles of water and extinguished, and weapons are tossed aside. In the middle of this quiet disarming, a series of shot-reverse-shots connects the twins to their parents, while slow-motion shots prolong the relief sweeping over Shaila and the twins as they run towards each other, weaving through the crowd. The soundtrack produces a rousing number, the final song 'Malarodi Malar Inghu/A Garland of Flowers', urging forgiveness and unity. From a high-angle shot, we see lost families reuniting, strangers holding each other's hands in a human chain that now binds them together, a Muslim girl and a Hindu man, and so on. Step-freeze editing that moves along the chain of clasped hands emphasises the utopian ending of communal harmony. In an adjacent space, we are not sure exactly how distant, Shaila and Shekhar are reunited with their boys. This structure of intercutting two spaces recalls the 'Humma, Humma' number, in which one scene informs the other. Here too, Shekhar and Shaila's intercommunal marriage informs narrative closure, in which the film returns to a civil society without the intervention of state power. It is here that the film's dealings with the events that besieged the city between December 1992 and April 1993 seem closer to cinematic yearnings and preoccupations than attempts to index them faithfully. Or, in other words, the closure to a family melodrama overwhelms the film's desire for verisimilitude; the cinematic convention of a song, the film suggests, is an option that is superior to surrendering to state law.

3 Final Images

Bombay closes with a freeze-frame of two images, a lap dissolve: a close-up shot of two hands joined together to signify the harmonious coexistence of communities, and a shot of the family of four huddled together against the backdrop of a ruined city A watery ending, limp in its politics and desire, I mused, thinking that either shot alone would have sufficed. I could not help raising the purpose of this last frame during my interview with Ratnam. Taking a look at the DVD image, he suggested that perhaps the outfit that produced the digital version had inadvertently compressed the images. He offered to look at the original frame on the editing table. The film was cued and ready for our inspection, and, to our surprise, his celluloid copy revealed a similar superimposed image. 'It should have been Edit-1,' he declared, explaining that one image, preferably the hands reaching out, should have been the final frame.

It is tempting to consider the final frame as a straightforward lapse in editing. Alternatively, we must remember that the audience, accustomed to dashing out of the theatre before the exits clog, rarely waits for the final frame. But close readings reanimate texts in different ways, and dwelling on the last frame is no exception. Rather than defer to authorial intention or even to Ratnam's mea culpa, I suggest that, having created a narrative dealing with traumatic incidents of communal violence by rendering them horrific, *Bombay* cannot draw the curtain with a simple resolution, even if the director wishes to.[83] The dissolve at the end of the film encourages us

The human chain in formation; the final dissolve

to read the gesture of communal harmony as a limited one despite the preceding sequence in which estranged families and communities are reunited: the spectre of communal violence is always proximate. It seems only fitting that, given the film's surreptitious pact with the horror genre, the final dissolve outwits Ratnam's rational intent. His sleight of hand vindicates the stubborn presence of the uncanny, evoking simultaneously the magic and science of cinema – deus ex machina.

Appendix

M-25062/33/1477

Endorsement No.II on Certificate No.91417-U dated the 01st MARCH, 1995 issued to the film 'BOMBAY'(TAMIL)COLOUR- 35mm - Cinemascope.

. . . . . .

Length Certified........3682.01 mts.in 14 Reels.

The applicant has made an addition of a song in Reel No.6(under rule 33) and the same has been seen and approved.

Length of the addition.......143.96 mts.

Actual length of the film after the above addition of a song will be......3825.97 mts. in 14 Reels.

Madras
Dated the 02nd MARCH,1995

for Chairman,
Central Board of Film Certification

ATTESTED THAT THE PARTICULARS IN THE CERTIFICATE INCLUDING AMENDMENT ARE CORRECT

Date

. . . . .

. . . . 3682.01 mts. in 14 reels.

M-25062

Endorsement on Certificate No. 91417-U dated the
01st MARCH, 1995. issued to the film 'BOMBAY'(TAMIL)
COLOUR - 35mm - CINEMASCOPE.

Cuts: ft   fr

General cut: Delete the words 'Pakistan',
             'Islamic State' and 'Afghanistan'   Sound
             wherever it occurs.   Deleted: only
             (Replaced with appd. words)

1. Reel 5   Delete the visuals of Rathyatra
             alongwith the dialogue 'Babri   Sound
             Masjid ihodenge Ram Mandir   only
             banayenge'.   Deleted:
             (Replaced with appd.dialogues)

2. Reel 7 (a) Delete the dialogues and visuals
              starting from 'Ayodiyile irrukkira
              Babar Majeedai idichu Raamar Koyil
              kattap poaram. Ovvur indhu veeti-
              lleyum panamo porulo vasool panroam.
              Masoodiyai idichu raamar koyil   Sound
              katta ungalaala mudincha uthavi   only
              sencheenganna nallayirukkum'.
                                     Deleted:
              (Replaced with appd. dialogues)

          (b) Delete all visuals of Babri
              Masjid and visuals of Babri   Visuals
              Masjid being pulled down.   super-
                                     Deleted: imposed.

          (c) Delete visuals of innocent
              persons(lady hanging clothes
              and person watching the riots   10   01
              from the balcony)being shot
              dead.   Deleted:

          (d) Delete the visuals of policeman
              lynched and another policeman
              brutally killed by the mob.   07   05
                                     Deleted:

3. Reel 7   Delete the visuals of policeman
             standing in file and shooting
             dead innocent persons with white   01   13
             caps on the road.   Deleted:

                                              .....2/-

: 2 :   M-25062
endorsement continued...

Cuts:			ft	fr
4. Reel 8	(a)	Delete the dialogue '25% minority community.Athaavathu muslims. Ungai policeukku enna muslimsnna pidikaatho' uttered by Sekar and also 'Irandhadhile 75% minority'. Deleted: (Replaced with appd.dialogues)	Sound only	
	(b)	Delete the dialogue 'Ayodhiyile masoodhiyai idichathukku yethirpaa ivanga kalavarathai aarambichaanga'uttered by the Inspector. Deleted: (Replaced with appd.dialogues)	Sound only	
5. Reel 10	(a)	Delete the dialogue 'Secularism perla yemaathitirukkira sarkar kitta kelunga'uttered by Sarkar Deleted:	12	02
	(b)	Delete the words 'Pakistan', 'Afghanistan','Islamic state','Muslim Naadu' wherever it occurs in this reel. Deleted:	07	00
	(c)	Delete the visuals and dialogues spoken by Tinu Anand while distributing Bangles.Deleted:	70	04
	(d)	Delete the visuals of Para-military men firing at a crowd with white cap on the ground. Deleted:	05	13
	(e)	Delete the dialogue of a person '500 varshangalukku mundadi ange oru kovil irunduchu. Adhai yaar idichathu.Ivangathaan Idhe muslimthaan'. Deleted:	34	13

.....3/-

: 3 :   M-25062

endorsement continued...

Cuts:			ft	fr
6. Reel 12	Delete the words 'Idhu Indhusthaan Paakistan illa' uttered by a Hindu. Deleted: (Replaced with appd.dialogues)		Sound only	
7. Reel 13	Reduce the scenes of violence by 25%. Reduced:		14	12
8. Reel 14	Delete the dialogue 'Muthalla avanga yelaaraiyum konnuttu appuram ingey vaanga'. Deleted: (Replaced with appd.dialogues)		Sound only	

163   13

(or)

49.96 mts.

Length applied.....3731.97 mts.

Length of cuts.....49.96 mts.

Actual length of the film after the above cuts

& replacements   will be.....3682.01 mts. in 14 Reels.

Madras   for Chairman,
Dated the 01st MARCH,1995 CENTRAL BOARD OF FILM CERTIFICATION

ATTESTED THAT THE PARTICULARS IN THE
CERTIFICATE INCLUDING ENDORSEMENT ARE CORRECT

Date   Regional Officer

2·3·95

Notes

1 *Bombay* was screened at the following festivals: Rotterdam, Hawaii International Film Festival, Indomania Festival in Paris, Toronto International Film Festival, Dublin, Asian Pacific Film and Video Festival in Los Angeles, Philadelphia Festival of World Cinema, Göteborg Film Festival in Sweden, Filmfest in Washington, D.C., National Film Theatre in London, Royal Tropical Institute in Amsterdam, Cinematica Portuguese in Lisbon, Bangkok International Film Festival, Espoo Cine Film Festival in Finland, Circulo De Bellas Artes in Madrid, and a retrospective of Mani Ratnam's films at the Calcutta Film Festival 2002.

2 For an evaluation of Mani Ratnam's impact on popular cinema after *Roja*, see Kavitha Shetty, 'A shooting success', *India Today*, 15 February 1994.

3 Bhawna Somaya, 'Unlocking dreams.' *The Hindu*, 30 December 1994.

4 For a racy biography of the city, see Suketu Mehta's *Maximum City: Bombay Lost and Found* (New York: Alfred A. Knopf, 2004).

5 E-mail communication with Mani Ratnam, 7 January 2005.

6 Two small-budget feature films also drawing on the communal events in a more circumspect manner are worthy of mention: *Zakhm/Wound* (1998) and *Naseem* (1995).

7 E-mail communication with Mani Ratnam, 7 January 2005.

8 Dileep Padgaonkar (ed.), *When Bombay Burned* (New Delhi: UBS Publishers, 1993).

9 Sivan subsequently directed his own film, *The Terrorist* (1999), which caught John Malkovich's eye at the Cairo Film Festival and became a sleeper at various international film festivals.

10 Interview with Rajiv Menon, Chennai, December 2003.

11 Santosh Vallury, interview with Mani Ratnam, *Stardust*, n.d.

12 G. S. Radhakrishnan, Gauri Lankesh and Sreedhar Pillai '*Bombay*: The Making of the Most Controversial Film of the Decade', *Sunday*, 2–8 April 1995, pp. 74–82.

13 Interview with Mani Ratnam, Chennai, December 2002.

14 Radhakrishnan, Lankesh and Pillai, '*Bombay*', p. 80.

15 Ibid., p. 81.

16 Ibid., p. 81.

17 Ibid., p. 81.

18 Ibid., p. 81.

19 'Censor Board is Obsolete: Interview with Mani Ratnam', Interview with Sandhya Rao, *Frontline*, 2 June 1995, pp. 128–30.

20 For a comprehensive account of this transition, see Sujata Patel, 'Bombay and Mumbai: Identities, Politics, and Populism', in Sujata Patel and Jim Masselos (eds), *Bombay and Mumbai: The City in Transition* (New Delhi: Oxford University Press, 2003), pp. 3–30.

21 All reports on screenings in Hyderabad are from 'Hyderabad Divided on *Bombay* ban', *Asian Age*, 17 March 1995, p. 3.

22 Additional details on Hyderabad from *Trade Guide*, vol. 41 no. 24, 18 March 1995, p. 15.

23 Hyderabad Divided', p. 3

24 Radhakrishnan, Lankesh and Pillai, '*Bombay*', p. 75.

25 Ibid.

26 *Trade Guide*, 8 April 1995.

27 'Bhopal Clears Bombay Release', *Asian Age*, 4 April 1995, p. 5.

28 Clarence Fernandez, 'Muslims to Protest against *Bombay* on Opening Day', *Asian Age*, 6 April 1995, p. 5.

29 *Trade Guide*, 8 April 1995.

30 Ibid., 4 April 1995.

31 'Bombay Stops *Bombay* for a Week', *Asian Age*, 8–9 April 1995, pp. 1, 4.

32 Ibid.

33 'Muslim Put Off Court Move on Film', *Asian Age*, 11 April 1995, p. 3.

34 'Maharashtra CM Says Film Must be Finally Released', *Asian Age*, 8–9 April 1995, p. 4.

35 'Muslim to Ask Joshi to Ban Film in Bombay', *Asian Age*, 13 April 1995, p. 3.

36 Ibid.

37 'Cheers Divide Audiences in Calcutta', *Asian Age*, 8–9 April 1995, pp. 1, 4.

38 Radhakrishnan, Lankesh and Pillai, '*Bombay*', pp. 81–2.

39 'Mani Ratnam Escapes Bomb Blast', *Trade Guide*, 15 July 1995.

40 'Manisha Koirala Receives Threatening Calls', *Trade Guide*, 5 August 1995.

41 *Trade Guide*, 8 April 1995.

42 Film Reviews, 1995–6, *Variety*.

43 Kavita Shanmugham', *Bombay* Takes the Romantic Road to Savagery', *Asian Age*, 21 March 1992, p. 12.

44 Poonam Saxena, '(…) is Washed with Love but There is also the Fire', *Asian Age*, 8 April 1995, no p. no.

45 C. Aravind, 'Ratnam Has the Courage to Voice His Convictions', *Asian Age*, 3 April 1995, p. 14.

46 Praful Bidwai, '*Bombay*: Fuss over Mediocrity', *Times of India*, n.d. or p. no.

47 Ibid.

48 Arun Sadhu, 'Clichés and Beyond', *Frontline*, 2 June 1995, pp. 131–2.

49 Venkatesh Athreya, 'Bold but Distorted', *Frontline*, 2 June 1995, pp. 132–3.

50 Georgekutty A. L. 'The Sacred, the Secular and the Nation in *Bombay*', *Deep Focus*, vol. 6, 1996, pp. 77–81.

51 Ibid., p. 80.

52 Shohini Chaudhuri and Howard Finn, 'The Open Image: Poetic Realism and the New Iranian Cinema', *Screen*, vol. 44 no.1, Spring 2003, pp. 38–57.

53 Ibid., p. 38.

54 Ibid., pp. 40, 55.

55 Ibid., p. 41.

56 Ravi S. Vasudevan, '*Bombay* and its Public', *Journal of Arts and Ideas*, no. 29, pp. 44–65.

57 'Screen Love Affair has Bombay up in Arms', *Independent*, 8 April 1995, pp. 12–13.

58 For a sampling, see Carol Clover, *Men, Women, and Chainsaws: Gender in the Modern Horror Films* (London: BFI, 1992); Rhona Berenstein, *Attack of the Leading Ladies: Gender, Sexuality, and Spectatorship in Classic Horror Cinema* (New York: Columbia University Press, 1996); Mark Janovich, *Horror: The Film Reader* (London: Routledge, 2002).

59 For a review of contemporary horror films in India, see Sandeep Unnithan and Kaveree Bamzai, 'Return of the Horror Show', *India Today*, 23 June 2003, pp. 42–8.

60 I wish to thank Earl Jackson Jr for his insights on *Dil Se*. Global/Local Conference, Honolulu, Hawaii, November 2003.

61 For a delightful reading of horror in Georges Franju's films, see Adam Lowenstein, 'Film Without a Face: Shock Horror in the Cinema of Georges Franju', *Cinema Journal*, vol. 37 no. 4, 1998, pp. 37–58.

62 Ofer Eliaz, 'From Beyond the Frame: Narrative Framing and the Figure of the Zombie in Romero's *Night of the Living Dead*', Master's thesis, Georgetown University, June 2000.

63 Thanks to Nasreen Munni Kabir for reminding me of this intertextual detail.

64 For a thorough discussion of the Steadicam, see Serena Ferrara, *Steadicam: Techniques and Aesthetics* (Oxford: Focal Press, 2001). Garrett Brown has written several articles on how to operate the Steadicam; for a sampling, see Garrett Brown, 'The Steadicam and *The Shining*', *American Cinematographer*, vol. 6 no. 8, August 1980, pp. 786–9, 826–7, 850–4.

65 Jean-Pierre Geuens, 'Visuality and Power: The Work of the Steadicam', *Film Quarterly* vol. 47 no. 2, 1993, pp. 8–17.

66 'Steadicam Cinematographers' Dream Comes True', *Screen*, 9 March 1984.

67 Personal interview with Chetan Shah, Chennai, December 2003.

68 Personal interview with Ramgopal Varma, Mumbai, December 2003.

69 Personal interview with Rajiv Menon, Chennai, December 2003.

70 Personal interview with Rajiv Menon, Chennai, December 2003.

71 Borrowing Paul Brass's careful differentiation between riots, violent acts and pogroms, I suggest that, with the arrival of the police, the uproar by Muslims in response to attacks on Babri Masjid is transformed from random acts of violence to the category of the riot – a distinct reaction to the state's inability to deliver justice or uphold law and order. Paul Brass, *Theft of an Idol: Text and Context in the Representation of Collective Violence* (Princeton, NJ: Princeton University Press, 1997).

72 For an analysis of censorship and pleasure, please see my discussion on 'Avenging Women in Indian Cinema', in Lalitha Gopalan, *Cinema of Interruptions: Action Genres in Contemporary Indian Cinema* (London: BFI, 2002).

73 Ravi S. Vasudevan, 'The Exhilaration of Dread: Genre, Narrative Form and Film Style in Contemporary Urban Action Films', in *Sarai Reader 02: The Cities of Everyday Life*, pp. 59–67.

74 For a newspaper account of this incident, see Clarence Fernandez and Naresh Fernandez, 'A city at War with Itself', in *When Bombay Burned*, Padgaonkar (ed.), pp. 42–5.

75 According to Menon, 'Step-freeze involves freezing every frame or every alternate frame for three to four frames. It dilates time but also makes the movements jerky, it worked in the case of *Bombay*.'

76 This incident, too, has been recorded in the newspapers as one that erupted in a predominantly Muslim slum in Jogeshwari, Padgaonkar (ed.), *When Bombay Burned*, pp. 48–51.

77 Erik Barnouw and S. Krishnaswamy, *Indian Film* (New York: Oxford University Press, 1980), p. 69.

78 See a series of articles by Bhaskar Chandravarkar, 'The Tradition of Music in Indian cinema', *Cinema in India*, vol. 1 no. 2, April 1987, to vol. 3 no. 3, July–September 1989; Ashok Ranade, 'The extraordinary importance of the Indian Film Song', *Cinema Vision India*, vol. 1 no. 4, 1981, pp. 4–11; S. Theodore Baskaran, 'Songs in Tamil Cinema', *The Eye of the Serpent* (Madras: East-West Books, 1996), pp. 38–61.

79 Interview with Ratnam, Chennai, December 2002.

80 These innovative interventions place Ratnam squarely in a genealogy beginning with Guru Dutt, who, according to Darius Cooper, was deeply committed to 'song situations' while being simultaneously engaged in genre cinema. See Darius Cooper, 'Hindi Film Song and Guru Dutt', *East-West Film Journal*, vol. 2 no. 2, 1988, pp. 49–65. Cooper, too, charts five situations: the wooing in the woods sequence; the cabaret/nightclub number; solitary song of remorse; festival song; fantasy song (p. 52).

81 Srinivas Bhashyam describes the editing of this sequence as a magical transformation from a sentimental number during the shoot into a heady metaphoric sequence.

82 See Vasudevan's reading of *Bombay* and this scene. Vasudevan, 'Bombay and its Public'.

83 For a delightful discussion of ghosts and dissolves in early photography, see Tom Gunning, 'Phantom Images and Modern Manifestations: Spirit Photography, Magic Theater, Trick Films, and Photography's Uncanny', in Patrice Petra (ed.), *Fugitive Images: From Photography to Video* (Bloomington: Indiana University Press, 1995), pp. 42–71.

Credits

Bombay

India
1995

Direction
Mani Ratnam
Producer
S. Sriram
Story/Screenplay
Mani Ratnam
[Hindi] Dialogue
Umesh Sharma
Cinematography
Rajiv Menon
Editing
Suresh Urs
Art
Thotta Tharani
Music
A. R. Rahman
Tamil Lyrics
Vairamuthu
Hindi Lyrics
Mehboob

Production Companies
Jhamu Sughand presents an
Aalayam Cinema (P) Ltd
production
An Aalayam presentation
An Amitabh Bachchan
Corporation Ltd release
Production Executive
J. Mohan
Production Manager
S. Sudhakar
Office Managers
S. Prabhakaran
T. K. Kumaravelan
Assistants
Raju
Marugan
Associate Director
U. V. Pani
1st Assistant Directors
B. Raveendra
Alagam Perumal - N.

2nd Assistant Directors
T. B. Srinivas
Susi Ganesan
Manoj
Daya Muthuraman
Kathiravan
2nd Unit Cameraman
Ganesh
Steadicam Operator
Prasad
Assistant Cameramen
R. D. Rajasekhar
P. Nagendran
R. Rathnavel
Anil Sekhar
Gopinath
Focus Pullers
Ravi
Gaja
Still Photography
Murali - Suresh
Assistant Still Cameramen
Jeeva
Annadurai
Assistants to Art Director
Thotta Yadhu
Jamal
(Production)
Assistants On-set
Raju
Kathir
Veeraswamy
Art Co-ordinators
sets: Thukaram
painting: Narayanan
moulding: Srinivasan
Costume Designer
Nalini Sriram
Dress Men
Seenu
Wardrobe
Shyam
Bujji
Make-up Artist
R. Sundara Moorthy
Assistant Make-up Men
Balaram
Nandagopal
Hair Stylist
Mohan
Choreography
Raju Sundaram
Prabhu Deva

Titles
Kambam Shankar
Optical Special F/X
(Prasad Productions (P) Ltd)
M. A. Hafiz
S. A. Azeem
Printed/Processed at
Prasad Film Laboratories
Song and Dance
Sequences (Tamil Version)
Kannalane
Playback Singer:
Chitra
Choreography:
Raju Sundaram
Uyire
Playback Singers:
Hariharan
Chitra
Humma Humma
Playback Singer:
Remo Fernandes
Choreography:
Prabu Deva
Halla gulla
Playback Singers:
Anupama
Malguddi Subha
Kuchi Kuchi
Playback Singers:
Hariharan
Swarnalata
Master G.V. Prakash
Choreography:
Raju Sundaram
Anna Bhoomi
chorus
Malarodi Mala
Playback Singers:
Sujatha
chorus
Songs (Hindi Version)
Kehna Hi Kya; *Tu Hi Re*;
Dil Hua Hai Deewana;
Kuchi Kuchi Rakrna;
Humma, Humma;
Ruk Jao, Ruk Jao (Riot)

Play Back Artistes
(Hindi Version)
Hariharan
Udit Narayan
Remo Fernandes
Kavita Krishnamurthy
Chitra
Pallavi
Anupama
Shuba
Noeli
Srinivas
Master G.V. Prakash
Sharada
Cassettes/CD's on
MIL - Music India (Polygram)
Dubbing/Mixing
V. S. Murthy
A. S. Lakshmi
Songs/(Background Score)
Re-recording
H. Sridhar
S. Sivakumar
Sound Editor
Shivanand
Assistant
Harsha
Audio Special F/X
A. S. Lakshmi
Assisted by
R. Ravichandran
Sethu
Sound Assistants
P. Saravanan
S. R. Subbaiah
T. Ramesh
G. N. Rao
T. K. Anbu
Catering In-charge
T. V. Muthu Krishnan
Ganesan
Spot Boys
Manohar
A. S. Chinnappa
Rajendran
V. Nagaraj
Leelammal

Transport
A. Siva
Babu
G. Ravi
M. Sekhar
Out Door Equipment
Anand Cine Service
Action (Stunt) Co-ordinator
Arun Patil
Action (Stunts)
Ravi Dewan
Publicity Designers
Media Men

Cast
Arvind Swamy
Shekhar
Manisha Koirala
Shaila Banu
Tinnu Anand
Shakti Samaj leader
Akash Khurana
Muslim leader
Nazar
T. Narayana Pillai
Kitty
Basheer Ahmed
Master Harsha
Kamal Basheer
Master Hriday
Kabir Narayana
guest appearances
Sonali Bendre
S. Nagendra Prasad
supporting cast
Ratnakar
Prakash Rai
Vasudeva Rao
Venkatesh
Raallapalli
Deesh Mariwala
Vinay Malhotra
Pramod Menon
Arun
A.R.S.
Vijaya Chandrika
Radha Bai
Sheila
Minu Rathod
Padmini Natarajan
Sreesha
Priya

12,724 feet
141 minutes

In Colour

Released in Hindi and Tamil
versions

Telugu title: *Bombayi*

Credits compiled by Julian
Grainger and Lalitha Gopalan

Also Published

Amores Perros
Paul Julian Smith (2003)

L'Argent
Kent Jones (1999)

Blade Runner
Scott Bukatman (1997)

Blue Velvet
Michael Atkinson (1997)

Caravaggio
Leo Bersani & Ulysse Dutoit (1999)

A City of Sadness
Bérénice Reynaud (2002)

Crash
Iain Sinclair (1999)

The Crying Game
Jane Giles (1997)

Dead Man
Jonathan Rosenbaum (2000)

Dilwale Dulhaniya Le Jayenge
Anupama Chopra (2002)

Don't Look Now
Mark Sanderson (1996)

Do the Right Thing
Ed Guerrero (2001)

Easy Rider
Lee Hill (1996)

The Exorcist
Mark Kermode (1997, 2nd edn 1998, rev. 2nd edn 2003)

Eyes Wide Shut
Michel Chion (2002)

Groundhog Day
Ryan Gilbey (2004)

Heat
Nick James (2002)

The Idiots
John Rockwell (2003)

Independence Day
Michael Rogin (1998)

Jaws
Antonia Quirke (2002)

L.A. Confidential
Manohla Dargis (2003)

Last Tango in Paris
David Thompson (1998)

The Matrix
Joshua Clover (2004)

Nosferatu – Phantom der Nacht
S.S. Prawer (2004)

Once Upon a Time in America
Adrian Martin (1998)

Pulp Fiction
Dana Polan (2000)

The Right Stuff
Tom Charity (1997)

Saló or The 120 Days of Sodom
Gary Indiana (2000)

Seven
Richard Dyer (1999)

The Shawshank Redemption
Mark Kermode (2003)

The Silence of the Lambs
Yvonne Tasker (2002)

10
Geoff Andrew (2005)

The Terminator
Sean French (1996)

Thelma & Louise
Marita Sturken (2000)

The Thing
Anne Billson (1997)

The Thin Red Line
Michel Chion (2004)

The 'Three Colours' Trilogy
Geoff Andrew (1998)

Titanic
David M. Lubin (1999)

Trainspotting
Murray Smith (2002)

Unforgiven
Edward Buscombe (2004)

The Usual Suspects
Ernest Larsen (2002)

The Wings of the Dove
Robin Wood (1999)

Withnail & I
Kevin Jackson (2004)

Women on the Verge of a Nervous Breakdown
Peter William Evans (1996)

WR – Mysteries of the Organism
Raymond Durgnat (1999)